To mum, dad and Helen.
The best family a girl
could ever wish for.

With love.

TOP DOG

Kate Bendix

Photography by Tiffany Mumford

Illustrations by Rupert Fawcett

Contents

Introduction p6

1 Dog + human = (joy + love)^2 p12

2 Now what's for dinner? p34

3 How to keep your dog in good health p90

4 Let your dog be a dog p184

5 So that's that p218

Top Dog selfies p224

Index p229

Introduction

Dogs are a joy, no? They're magic little creatures to have about the place. A friendly, curious, mischievous beating heart of fur and claw. They will be your companion through good times and bad, will love you unconditionally and make you a healthier, happier person.

As a nation, we now own over nine million of the little blighters, and the number is rising. We're opting for smaller dogs over giant breeds, because they're cheaper to run; we live in ever smaller spaces, in more urban surroundings, and have busier lives. But we're fitting them in wherever we can and dogs are increasingly becoming a family member in their own right.

So, what's not to love? Dogs make us better, happier people. Everyone should have a dog!

Well, yes, but then again... Do you sometimes – just for a moment, in secret, of course – wonder whether you've bitten off more than you can chew? Is your

dog harder work than you thought she would be? Did she ruin your best rug with her impromptu peeing and pooing (mine did)? Do you wonder why, when the vet recommended a prescription-only diet food so expensive it's on a par with the GDP of a small country, your dog is getting even fatter? Or why, after successive rounds of antibiotics and steroids she's still got a bald back end?

Of course, we all want the best for our dogs, we want to do right by them, but when things go wrong we can only act in our dog's best interests using the information we have to hand.

And what out-dated and outmoded information that often is. Let's look at how your dog's world is wrapped up in everyone's bottom lines for a moment.

The food manufacturer recommends you feed your dog their food, and only that – for ever. The pharmaceutical companies would rather you treated your dog for parasites and diseases on a regular basis using *their* products. The vet wants you to make regular visits to their practice to keep sales up, the idea being that when the dog actually gets sick you can claim it back through your pet insurance company. But then because medical science has come on leaps and bounds, the cost of treatment is going through the roof; worse still, your dog has a disease needing lifetime medication, so your insurance premium has gone stellar.

While new medical treatments are welcome, many of them are being used on dogs who should never have got sick in

the first place because the disease they have developed was so avoidable.

I run a company called My Itchy Dog, giving advice on and supplying healthy supplements and treats for dogs, mainly with skin problems, but I spend a lot of time promoting healthy pet care too.

At My Itchy Dog we get loads of calls and emails seeking advice, and conversations often begin with this kind of half-panicky statement: 'Florence won't stop scratching. She's had antibiotics, steroids, skin scrapes and allergy testing, still scratching! She's had so much treatment I'm thinking of buying shares in my vet's practice... I'm at my wits' end, so I thought I'd call you.' Thanks!

I have written this book so that you can take back control of your pet's well-being. What I'm advocating is a manifesto for a new understanding of our canine friends – another way of having a dog, if you like – because, in my experience, there *is* another way. A better, less stressful way of rearing a dog who will stay happy and healthy for longer, and who will cost you less in the long run.

I promise you that, by following the methods in this book, making a few tweaks where necessary, you *can* have that dog.

But, before you go thinking this is all too good to be true, I'm going to be honest with you about what you won't find within these pages. You will not find a cure for cancer, a natural treatment for established heart disease or a cure for your dog's pancreatitis. You need to be working with your vet on those tricky beggars, and good luck to you, I wish you well. What you will find is a method for helping your dog to avoid developing a preventable disease in the first place. It doesn't matter if you're thinking of getting a dog or have had one for years, it can still work. You can prevent heart disease, diabetes, cancers and obesity from taking hold and treat ailments like colitis, skin problems and recurring ear infections so they go away and stay away.

I know you can do it because I've done it – with our dogs.

Ronnie, our Bedlington terrier, gets flea allergies and comes up in sore, red and very itchy bumps when he gets bitten. BB, Bedlington number two, came to us as a three-year-old rescue in a bit of a state. She was fat, had greasy fur, was so unfit she couldn't make the stairs and was almost blind in her left eye, which wept continuously – and which the vet wasn't sure could be saved. She itched constantly, everywhere. Nikita, an abandoned dog found roaming the streets in Bulgaria, came to me without much fur, newly treated mange, ongoing malasseezia (a fungal skin infection), skinny, and with teeth that had lost most of their enamel. We thought she was a chihuahua cross.

We treated them all holistically, and do to this day. We changed BB's diet. Ronnie got the neem oil shampoo treatment. We added echinacea and a herbal blend for digestion to BB's and Nikita's food, along with omega oils, and treated their skin with neem oil shampoo and a soothing coconut lotion. We put all of them onto herbal flea, tick and mite treatment and Verm-X herbal worming treats. And over the next six months this is what happened.

Ronnie no longer got bitten. BB lost all her excess weight, her coat grew out to be lovely and soft, she learned to run, started to get to grips with the stairs and stopped weeing all over the house. And she didn't lose the eye. Nikita put on a kilo, her skin healed, she grew fur, and developed a cheeky personality that makes me laugh every day. And she turned out to be a collie cross, with probably Jack Russell/chihuahua/Pomeranian leanings. We're not sure.

BB still scratches, but not nearly half as much, and we manage that as and when she has a flare up.

So if you have got a dog that's in need of a bit of TLC – if you've tried in vain to solve his gunky ears, if you want to find out why the food you feed him is probably responsible for most of his physical problems, if you have a dog who thinks it's acceptable to pee in your shoe and you can't for the life of you work out how to get him to stop... this book is for you.

Enjoy 🐾

'First one
back gets
to sit in the
front seat'

Dog + human = (joy + love)^2

So you think you want a dog...

This section is a little digression for all of you who can't resist giving every dog you meet a wistful scratch behind the ears – an important bit of small print for you to read and absorb *before* you acquire a Rufus or Sally of your very own. (Those of you who already have a dog may want to skip this bit, though there should be quite a lot in it to interest you, too: perhaps you are thinking of getting a new puppy, a companion for Fido? Or perhaps there are things you would like to do differently in the future...)

If you're planning to get a dog, you must ask yourself 'What are my reasons?' Before you head on down to the rescue centre or even think about contacting a breeder, make sure you can answer this question: Why do you want a dog?

Six little words hanging in the air, like drool from a St Bernard's jowls.

Because, let's face it, owning and looking aftera dog is a huge responsibility, almost like having a child. Like kids, they don't come with a manual and no one will admit how much work they really are until you get one. The smaller they are the longer they live, so you could easily be looking at a 15-year commitment to a creature that will never get past the age of two, mentally and emotionally speaking, will never contribute to your old age and will more than likely cause you a tear or two.

And, if you think of everything you need

to do for a child, it's the same for a dog. You can't leave them alone in the house, certainly not for long periods of time. Imagine the havoc that would be caused by of a couple of two-year-olds left to their own devices with snacks and crayons, in your living-room or kitchen... Dogs are no different, if you don't count opposable thumbs, and they can do a fair bit of damage with those claws and jaws.

Dogs are intelligent, sentient beings liable to boredom and frustration. Just like the rest of us. They need stuff to DO!

So say bye bye to your freedom. Adios to an immaculate house. Au revoir to spontaneity – unless you've got great dog-sitters. While babies are allowed in cafes, restaurants, museums, shops, doctors' surgeries, schools and playgrounds, dogs are not. Granted, you can't put kids on a lead, but a dog on a lead is still very much with you. Every day.

And it may sound unnecessary at this stage to point this out, but I feel I must do it anyway.... *a dog is not a cat!*

Cats are attached to places and are generally fine so long as their home space is settled and secure. My cat Pearl only cares that I live long enough to feed her each day, but if there's something going on in the house, especially if it involves power tools, she's over the fence and won't come back till sundown.

A dog is attached to her 'person', some breeds more than others, but basically all dogs need people, love, stimulation and interaction. And that's what you need to consider when you're thinking about getting one. How much time and effort are you prepared to put into your dog to make him into a respectable member of society, a pleasure to hang out with?

I'm not kidding when I say that adding a dog to your life is going

to change it dramatically. Depending on the breed you choose, he may need a lot of walking, or only a short 45-minute walk in the morning followed by a few 'comfort' walks for the rest of the day. It's still time out of your day and it doesn't mean he can be ignored for the rest of the time either.

You may be shouting out right now, 'Kate, stop patronising me! I know what it takes to look after a dog, I had them when I was a kid.' So did I. We had a black Lab, a Lab puppy and a German shepherd. We lived in a pub, in Battersea, in the 70s. Believe me, that was a time and a place you needed a dog! At least living above the pub meant we were always in, so they weren't left alone all day. I was only six when we got Fred, the Lab puppy. At that age I never had to walk our dogs, or feed them, or look out for their welfare or pay their vets' bills. I wasn't the person who had to make the decision to put the German shepherd (Ben) down when he developed distemper, or give Fred away to people who could give him the time he needed, and deserved. As it was, he was never trained properly. I think the end was in sight when he chewed up a box of toilet rolls and left the

'Frisbee!
Yeah, baby!'

bits all over the flat. That and the pooing. Hey, it was the 70s, and my mum was probably just trying to keep me, my sister and my dad in check, never mind the dog. We got left asleep in the back of the car at motorway service stations at night while they went for a cuppa, so the dog had no chance. Doesn't excuse it, though. Fred needed time spent on him, only there wasn't any.

And the reason I get on my soap-box about really thinking it over, seriously, before you get a dog, is that you are going to saddle yourself with a being who will need feeding, exercising, grooming, playing with and cuddling for a very long time.

Until 2004, we had a gorgeous rescue lurcher, the darling Bud, who would happily run about for an hour in the morning then take up residence on the sofa or, conveniently, in the hallway so you had to step over him every time you wanted to pass, for the rest of the day. And, if it was raining, good luck to you getting him out the door for a pee later on. Wasn't happening. Equally he would happily go for a two- or three-hour hike, sniffing around the trees, chasing rabbits. He needed exercise, but it wouldn't take up your whole day. Whereas Judy, our Jack Russell, needed running practically into the ground! And if we didn't stop her in time, she'd leg it down a rabbit-hole and be lost to us for up to a day. She had to be dug out a few times.

So, ask yourselves one more time: would you leave a child alone in the house all day? Would you leave him or her tied up outside a shop? Didn't think so. Would you leave a kid in the back of your car while you went to work, getting anyone you could blag off to walk her at lunchtime? My old boss did, and thanks to a couple of us being such dog lovers she got a good walk, but it was cruel behaviour on his part. When he got a new girlfriend the dog was rehomed. She was a lovely rescue greyhound, loyal to a fault. Because she was a dog. And they are a loyal species. It's how they've survived this long and ingratiated themselves into our hearts and lives.

The plus side, though, is that if you put the effort in at the beginning, a dog will give you great reward (at far less cost than a child!) House-training is quicker; you can take steps to avoid unwanted pregnancy; and you can leave a dog alone for a couple of hours at a younger age, while you go shopping.

Just remember: you have the control. The dog doesn't. Don't assume it lightly. Treat the dog and the responsibility with the respect they command. Sermon over.

The benefits of owning a dog

I've looked for peer-reviewed research into the benefits to human health of owning a dog. There's surprisingly little out there on the subject; most papers discuss why there is barely any research in evidence and how most of the advantages of owning a dog are anecdotal. However, I know I am not alone in thinking that the health benefits of owning a dog are legion and very real.

Depression and mood

As someone who suffers from depression, quite badly on occasion, I can honestly say that getting a dog has improved my mood and overall outlook no end. I've missed weddings, job interviews and dates because I was depressed. The Black Dog (how ironic) has nailed me to the sofa for weeks at a time on a couple of occasions. My friend Sophie says that when I'm bad it's like someone's turned the lights off behind my eyes. The dead shark stare, as Ruby Wax calls it.

So I take antidepressants, talk about it, make sure I get enough sleep, avoid stress when I can and try mindfulness as a way of managing it. But my best and most powerful tool in the drawer is being with my dog. She has such a significant effect on that part of me that I wrote a blog post about it on my website www.myitchydog. co.uk and it's the most read post I've ever put up there. It's had thousands of hits and many comments. People know what I'm talking about; they've had the same experiences.

Taking responsibility for a dog, making sure she's OK and her needs are being met, can really boost self-esteem, when your stores of self-confidence are at their lowest. Looking after a dog, feeling the unconditional love she lavishes upon you, the fact that she's pleased to see you no matter what state you're in or how bad your day has been is an immediate mood-booster. You can't stay in with a box-set and a whole chocolate cake for company. The dog needs a walk. Walking outside in the fresh air – even just a twirl around the park – raises your spirits, gets you off the sofa and moving. You can't walk, throw a stick for the dog, comfort-eat and weep copiously at the same time. Believe me, I've tried!

Owning a dog reduces the isolation and loneliness duvet we tend to wrap ourselves in when we're down. I can't walk up the road, over the Downs or along the beach without having at least one conversation with someone, usually a total stranger. Dogs offer us touch, too, without expectation that they'll get any back. I defy you to lie in bed with your dog by your side, wedging his wriggly little bum into the small of your back, and not feel a moment of joy, even just a teeny tiny one.

Dogs shine a beam of light upon us, and the world seems a far duller place when they're not by our side.

Walkies!

When you've got a dog, no matter what the weather's doing, unless it's truly biblical outside, you're going out. And, as

> Regular exercise, such as walking your dog, lowers blood pressure, cholesterol and blood sugar levels, reduces stress, aids weight loss and also improves mood and sleep patterns.

with all exercise, the minute you're doing it, you're thinking, 'Why don't I do this more often?' or 'It's such a lovely day.' The benefits of exercise are very well documented, whether you're doing it with or without a pooch by your side. Having a dog you must exercise makes it much easier and far more enjoyable. It also turns you into a bit of a mate magnet too. Friends who normally can't be bothered turn up at your door and ask, 'Do you and Nikita want to come out for a walk?' (they really mean Nikita; I'm just a by-product of her popularity) because they know it makes them feel better too.

Confidence-building in children

Dogs really are a child's best friend. Who can you talk to when your parents just don't get it? The dog of course! The dog listens, she understands you, and she's not too busy making your dinner, washing your clothes or earning the money to keep a roof over your head (selfish parents!) to spend time lounging on your bed and listening to your gripes and worries. Talking things over with the family dog reduces stress and allows children to develop the skill of working things out for themselves.

Helping to take care of the dog also boosts a child's self-confidence and teaches her responsibility; teaching the dog new tricks will strengthen the bond between dog and child too, creating a friendship she will remember for ever.

Don't go with the flow

For maximum enjoyment and fulfilment, really do your research before you decide which breed to go for. This applies both to getting a puppy from a breeder and adopting a rescue from a centre – Dogs Trust, for example. Whatever you do, please don't buy a dog from an unknown source online, from a puppy farm or from an ad in the paper, on Preloved or Gumtree. Puppies bought from those places are often bred on puppy farms. The poor bitches are bred continuously in horrendous conditions then disposed of when their 'useful' life has ended.

Deciding which breed of dog you want should depend on the life you have now, what you can afford and how much you want to get up to with your dog. For instance, if you live in or have access to open spaces and like to walk and stay active, then a dog that needs more exercise is a great option. If you're really into agility (or would like to be) or flyball, a collie, terrier or spaniel will be your best companion, whereas a bichon frise would just as likely look you up and down while not moving a muscle. If you like the quiet life or work outside the home all day, then you want a breed that is content to spend a couple of hours at a time on his own, with someone coming in to walk and interact with him while you're out all day. Or happy to be at doggy day care, or able to come to work with you.

What I'm getting at is this: please don't choose a dog breed based on fashion, celebrity or nostalgia. The dog you had as a kid was around in a different time and won't necessarily suit your adult life. As for celebrities, they pay people to look after their dogs, and don't think they don't make a massive gaffs in choosing their breed either. A husky needs something to *do* – it's not all cute eyes and thick fur; those dogs are seriously strong and they need to work, not stare at the walls all day.

Celebrity, *Game of Thrones* and a bad press are the reasons dog rescue centres are overflowing with Staffordshire bull terriers, huskies and malamutes right now. If you don't believe that we're swayed by fashion, just as much when choosing a dog as a new kitchen, have a look at the piece of research overleaf.

While retrievers are still the most popular breed by far, what I find most interesting is the Kennel Club data in the far right column of this chart. Look at the increases and decreases in registrations of new puppies by breeders from 1999 to 2008. You can see clearly that Yorkshire terriers, Westies and Rottweilers have fallen out of fashion in favour of other, often much smaller breeds: Border terriers – up 138%; and miniature schnauzers up 142%, for example. But look at the figure for pugs – a 524% increase in new registrations! That's fashion, pure and simple.

Consider the Obamas' dog, Bo, a Portuguese water dog born in 2008, when there were 74 Kennel Club registrations for the breed. In 2013 there were 195. So, a large, working dog who needs quite a bit to do, a capacious house and daily grooming is the dog of choice for people who want a dog 'like the Obamas' one'. Or, if you're a Reese Witherspoon or Hugh Jackman fan, you may have set your heart on a French bulldog. In 2004 there were 350 registrations of French bulldog puppy litters with the Kennel Club; in 2013 that figure was (wait for it) 6990, nearly a 20-fold increase. We are definitely dedicated followers when it comes to doggie fashion.

Popularity of breeds from micro-chip records and UK Kennel Club registrations

Breed	% micro-chip registered dogs	% of KC registrations
Unknown	23.37	
Cross	12.6	
Retriever (Labrador)	9.96	16.4
Staffordshire bull terrier	4.92	3.9
German shepherd dog (Alsatian)	4.22	4.32
Border collie	4.21	0.86
Spaniel (cocker)	3.49	8.16
Spaniel (English springer)	3.39	5.4
Yorkshire terrier	2.49	1.43
Retriever (Golden)	2.48	3.32
West Highland white terrier	2.48	2.66
Cavalier King Charles spaniel	2.01	4.07
Rottweiler	1.57	0.95
Border terrier	1.46	3.32
Shih-tzu	1.25	1.99
Boxer	1.04	2.67
Lhasa apso	0.86	1.86
Poodle	0.83	1.31
Bichon frise	0.7	1
Greyhound	0.63	0.02
Weimaraner	0.63	0.83
Dalmatian	0.6	0.57
Miniature schnauzer	0.6	1.93
Dachshund	0.60	1.98
Bulldog	0.54	1.65
Chihuahua	0.53	2.57
Bull terrier	0.49	1.06
Whippet	0.48	1.21
Pug	0.29	1.62
King Charles spaniel	0.28	0.07

Micro-chip breed popularity rank *	KC popularity rank (2008)	% increase in KC registrations (1999-2008)
1	1	35.44
2	6	8.53
3	4	-33.52
4	26	25.59
5	2	68.25
6	3	20.07
7	17	-46.16
8	7	-28.05
9	10	-49.16
10	5	-3.03
11	23	-50.41
12	8	138.84
13	11	45.33
14	9	-25.68
15	14	61.22
16	21	-0.66
17	22	13.27
18	163	17.95
19	27	-4.75
20	37	-40.99
21	13	142.19
22	12	1.47
23	15	115.72
25	18	-18.80
27	20	11.02
28	19	104.80
37	16	524.83
38	105	15.38

* not including unknown and cross-breeds.

CANINE THERAPY

The Kennel Club has started a 'Bark and Read' programme to help improve the literacy of children, especially those with emotional and behavioural difficulties and it's proving to be a roaring success. A dog will visit a school so that the children can practise reading to it. Dogs are non-judgmental and attentive listeners and research has shown that children who practise reading to a dog sitting beside them become better readers, and gain more confidence about reading aloud in class, or just speaking out in general.

TRY BEFORE YOU BUY

A good way to put your toe in the water, so to speak, for those of you who have some experience with dogs would be to volunteer to walk dogs at your local rescue, or to help care for someone else's dog when they need help (the Cinnamon Trust always need dog walkers, short-term carers and fosterers). All require different levels of commitment but it's a great way of finding out just what having a dog in your life entails.

www.dogstrust.org.uk
www.cinnamon.org.uk

TOOLS TO HELP YOU DECIDE

There are some great 'choose your pet' calculators online. They're mostly very simple, but then a dog's needs are pretty simple: **location, exercise, money and time.**

Try these:
http://www.pdsa.org.uk/pet-health-advice/your-right-pet – this site will help you work out which type of pet is right for you.

http://animal.discovery.com/breed-selector/dog-breeds.html – will determine the dog breeds to those that best suit your lifestyle based on the ten simple questions you answer. It's also got a great section where you can look at breeds based on your wants i.e. family dogs, herding dogs, hunting dogs, energetic dogs, etc.

'What shall we do now?'

Do you want a brand new dog, or a rescue?

Breeds are a contentious issue with many, as they're generally bred in the interests of the show crowd and its competitors, or in the interests of fashion and market forces, but not those of the dog. When you are choosing which kind of dog is right for you, don't forget the money/time spent section of your checklist: what inherited health problems is this breed likely to come with? How much will it cost me to keep on top of the these issues? And do I want that? West Highland white terriers are susceptible to skin problems; spaniels to ear infections, unsurprisingly; German shepherds to hip problems; and chihuahuas, pugs and, Boston terriers to eye problems.

Think about your life and how a dog will fit into it. Do your research. If you can't get to a Discover Dogs show or something similar, the Kennel Club should have a list of registered breeders on their books.

'We'll get a puppy because we don't know where a rescue has come from.'

That's one of the most common lines I hear when friends, especially those with children, are thinking about getting a dog. 'We won't know the rescue's history, and we feel a puppy would be cute!' Doubtless they're right, about the cute part anyway, but puppies are work! They're babies. The question is how much time do you have to train a puppy? Some are harder work than others – though, having said that, all dogs will require some training.

Of course, you want whichever dog you take on to be good around the kids, but that's got a lot to do with which breed you go for, where he has come from, his age, your kids' ages and behaviour and how much you're prepared to integrate your dog into the family. You must be prepared to train the children as well as the dog.

It isn't, in fact, always the case that you won't know the history of a rescue dog. If you make enquiries at a rescue centre they'll want to know a fair bit about your family set-up and your lifestyle so that they're not setting you and the dog up to fail. Not every dog that's ever passed through the doors of Battersea or Dogs Trust has been abused or badly treated in some way. Often these days dogs have been given up because the owners simply can't afford their upkeep any longer, or they've become too ill to care for them or passed away. Some dogs will be used to families and kids, some to old ladies, single households or other pets and the rescue centre will pair you up with the right dog for you. So don't decide until you've had a good exploratory chat. Plus, a rescue could well be the breed of your choice and you won't be a thousand pounds lighter for it either!

What a dog needs

Dogs need the basics: food, water, a comfy bed to call their own, love, safety and shelter.; boundaries and leadership; socialisation and a sense of belonging; attention and affection; physical exercise, training and psychological challenges.

They do not need: to be left alone all day, to be carried about in a bag, dressed up, married off to other dogs or given birthday parties which you invite all their other doggy friends to.

Believe it or not, as a dog owner you have legal obligations to any dog in your care. There is a code of conduct, wrapped up in the Welfare of Animals Act 2006 (amended in 2013) which sets out the five basic needs of a dog – needs which you, as the dog's guardian, must provide as a minimum standard of care. They are:

1. The need for a suitable environment

2. The need for a suitable diet

3. The need to be able to exhibit normal behaviour patterns

4. The need to be housed with, or apart from, other animals

5. The need to be protected from pain, suffering, injury and disease

Let's expand a bit on each one:

1. The need for a suitable environment. A dog's physical needs inside your home need to be considered carefully. A dog needs her own space, somewhere she can retreat to when she needs to sleep, relax, or to get away from noise, sticky-fingered children or the hoover. It could be her own bed, your own bed, a dog crate, or a quiet corner of a quiet room. Somewhere she can feel safe and secure, free from the threat of harm.

2. The need for a suitable diet – are you willing, and financially able to provide the best food you can for a dog? Can you do the research, take the time and effort to find out which is the best diet for his needs? Are you happy to give him a varied diet, to make food he likes and change his drinking water at least twice a day?

3. The need to be able to exhibit normal behaviour patterns. Dogs love to chew. Next to being out and about it's their best stress-reliever. Chewing, sniffing, being curious, socialising, playing with other dogs, chasing squirrels up trees, running as fast as they can and spending time with you are all normal behaviours for dogs. Being quiet all the time, being kept permanently on a lead out on a walk or living in a crate or in just one room in the house, apart from you, are definitely not normal behaviours for them. Can you provide the ongoing company, training, patience and toys a dog will need?

4. **The need to be housed with, or apart from, other animals.** Dogs love to play with other dogs – fact! They don't like all other dogs though. That's a bit like saying humans should get on with all other humans. It just doesn't happen. But dogs like nothing better than having a good play with other dogs they consider friends. Nikita can spot one of her mates from the other end of the park and takes off like a rocket to greet them. Equally, we need to keep them safe from harm and out of reach of dogs (and their owners) who could do our dogs harm because they're either not trained at all, or trained to be nasty in the first place. I always read the owners to determine this one.

5. The need to be protected from pain, suffering, injury and disease – your dog will need exercising by someone else when you can't. Your house will need dog-proofing so he doesn't end up in surgery getting knicker elastic extracted from his gut. You'll need to keep him free of parasites, in good physical shape and let him grow old gracefully. This day-to-day maintenance will be, by a country mile, your greatest expense in owning a dog. Have you got that kind of cash? Are you prepared to make the financial sacrifices to make sure that you do?

Being that selfless on behalf of another being takes work. A dog will pee and poo and barf in your house. Once in a while, when he's sick or being house-trained or you've locked him in the living room accidentally, he may well eat things he shouldn't, chew things that don't belong to him or fall asleep on that 'just back from the dry cleaners' little black dress you were going out in tonight, leaving his white fur behind. He just will. Are you ready for all that?

If the answer's yes, then hooray! Happy 'gotcha' day! It's a bit like getting the baby home from the hospital. All of a sudden you're responsible for this little creature and you definitely don't have enough of the stuff he needs...

Preparing your home, and yourself, for your new dog

So, you've taken the plunge and you're just hours away from welcoming a new addition to your home, and into your life. I was a bag of nerves when I got Nikita, and I had more than a month to prepare! I rushed around buying too much stuff: would she need a crate, do I get a hard bed I can line with blankets in case she's not house-trained? Or do I go for the full-on memory foam, fluffy-blanket-bed madness and sod the risk? Toys? Chews? Food? Just tell me what to get!!!!!

My advice? Chill out. Relax. The things you do need to have sorted fairly swiftly are: ID and micro-chip All dogs in the UK have to be micro-chipped by law. They also need to wear a collar with an ID tag. (Don't put the dog's name on the tag, otherwise she's easier to steal – because the dog is more likely to follow someone who gets her name right. Just put your surname and mobile number down and ask the finder to kindly call you.)

You will also need to have thought about her physical and psychological needs – to be able to provide a space to make her own for sleeping; a place where she knows she can pee; and a quiet introduction to the house and its occupants. A new dog should not be left on her own in the new house for a while until she's sure of her surroundings, boundaries etc. Getting a dog over a bank holiday weekend or when you're off work for a week or so would be good.

As for shopping for all the other paraphernalia, don't rush at any of it. Before your dog turns up you won't know what he or she even likes, and dogs do have preferences, believe me. Also, it's all new to them so they're generally on their best behaviour for a few weeks at least.

Another bit of advice I'd give, especially if it's your first dog or you haven't had one for years, is to have a dog-owning friend with you when you get your new dog. My good friend Helen O'Donnell was with me the first day I got Nikita. I remember sitting in the kitchen with Helen, chatting and really being nervous to the pit of my stomach. Was I doing the right thing? For me and for the dog? Could I manage this already badly treated dog, who was this minute winging her way down the M23, all the way from Bulgaria, on the front seat of a van (Nikita doesn't do the back)? Could I provide the home, care, love and attention she really needed? And totally deserved.

There was a knock at the front door, I opened it and there was Michelle from K9 Rescue Bulgaria, with Nikita, who looked, on the surface at least, all bouncy and happy. Happy to be out of the van on this hot day, happy to be outside, but half mad with stress, fatigue and confusion. Skin and bone, rough and greasy-coated.

THIS IS WHAT I BOUGHT BEFORE NIKITA CAME:

Moulded plastic dog bed

A dog crate

Blankets for the sofas

Raw food

Tinned food

Food in pouches

A new collar

A flexi-lead

Poo bags from the pet shop (scented, horrible things)

HERE'S WHAT I RETURNED, GAVE TO CHARITY OR EXCHANGED WITHIN THE FIRST TWO WEEKS:

Moulded plastic dog bed (charity) – lost £15

Dog crate (returned and refunded) – clawed back £65

Raw food (given to a friend's dog, Nikita just wasn't ready for it) – lost £20

Food in pouches (too rich for her – donated to a local rescue) – lost £10

The new collar (way too big! charity shop) – lost £8

HERE'S WHAT I BOUGHT WHEN I DISCOVERED WHAT I REALLY NEEDED:

A collar that fitted and a new short lead

A long lead (for letting her have some freedom while teaching her to come back to me)

Very smelly training treats – needed these from day one: 'I'm your friend, it's all good here, well done for peeing in the garden not on my rug' etc

A good harness because her neck is very thin and she chases things so I wanted better control and for her to be more comfortable

A seatbelt for her harness

A proper ID tag the right size for her

Food she could tolerate while I was getting some meat back on her bones

The right sized food and water bowls

A woolly, machine-washable dog bed from TK-Max for £10

A Stag Bar for her to chew and take out her stress on

Skin red with a fungal infection and nails badly in need of clipping. And my heart leapt at the sight of her, my nerves just vanished and she was mine. She rocked up to the front door, into the hallway, said hello to me and raced off through the house to the garden. You know I'm talking about the dog now, not Michelle, right?

So I'd say prepare the bare bones of what you and your dog need that first day. The shops will be open again tomorrow.

Helen and I took Nikita to the beach, her first time on sand, in rock pools and in the sea. She came upon a seagull almost as big as she was, and drank sea water out of a rock pool, which can't have been pleasant. But she'd just been dumped with two complete strangers and everything smelled funny, different, so she had no choice but to make the best out of the situation and put her best foot forward to make a good impression. So she did a really stressy, runny poo on the beach.

Atta girl!

Now, do you still want a dog?

If you consider all of the above, and think that what's necessary is doable and you still want a dog, then go forth, lovely human, and get yourself a furry, messy, sometimes smelly but always adorable and loyal companion.

I wonder if, after going through this chapter, you still fancy the breed you were after originally or if it's changed the way you think. Have you gone from husky to Jack Russell, or greyhound to Heinz 57 mutt? Whatever, as long as you've thought it through and are prepared for what you're letting yourself in for you've gone a long way to giving yourself the best opportunity for a long-lasting and loving relationship with your new-found friend.

If you get the basics right a dog will give you her unconditional love and be a happy member of your family who will contribute to your happiness and well-being in ways you cannot imagine.

'Are you going without me?'

Now what's for dinner?

The importance of diet

Don't underestimate just how crucial a healthy diet will be to your dog and to you. What you feed her will help determine how long she lives, the state of her health while she's alive and how long she will stay well. Remember, this crazy dog child of yours won't ever grow up and leave home, and there is no NHS for our pets. So feed them well, keep their immune system strong and enjoy your bouncy, healthy dog for much longer. You'll save money on vets' bills into the bargain. I guarantee it.

Somewhere along the line, it has become acceptable to feed our dogs the same food, over and over again, day in day out, for years. But why? Think about it: your dog lives, on average, to be 12 years old. You feed her twice a day. That's

8760 meals she's going to eat during his lifetime. Not including treats.

That's a lot of kibble. Let's take the average dog (I realise there is no such thing but work with me here). I'm going to get myself an average dog; I think I'll name him Charlie after my Auntie Lyn's Yorkshire terrier, lovely boy. Charlie weighs 25kg and, let's say I feed him dry food, roughly 375g a day. If he lives until he's 12, which he will because he's, y'know, 'average', that will be nearly 274 sacks of 12kg dog food. That's either a lot of good or a lot of bad food your dog will eat.

What if you were that dog? Try and envisage your own personal Groundhog Day. Imagine that you mosey on down to the kitchen every day from the comfort of your snuggly dog bed to dine out on... garbage. You love garbage; it's full of sugars, possibly added colours (which you can't see well because you're a dog, and don't see colours as vividly as a human), it's crunchy, though, and you like crunchy. Next you move on to the wet stuff. It's got some nice, tasting gravy going on there, but the 'chunks' of meat don't pose much of a challenge so it's soon dispatched and the bowl is licked clean. Yummers! Now, where's my bed?

That's all well and good when you're young – you can eat what you like and still party like it's 1999, stay out all night (if only you weren't locked in the kitchen) and get busy giving the other dogs the run-around in the park. No one catches the puppy! Having said that, your energy is a bit up and down, your skin itches and your ears are a bit gunky, but you can live with it.

Give it a few years of eating the same cheap (or even very expensive) dog food with the low-quality ingredients and you start to feel tired more easily. Your waistline has expanded. You don't smell fabulous either – could be your gut, could be your plaquey old teeth; no one's too sure. Your skin's itching so you constantly chew your paws, frustrating your human no end, and you could do without your anal glands being blocked up then manually squeezed empty by the vet. Oh, the humiliation! And because you're middle-aged and rotund your joints have started growling. Now you're not the fastest dog in the park any longer, but that's OK because you're about as energetic as, well, an overweight middle-aged dog fed a poor diet all its life.

Now don't take this personally. This is just an example of what Charlie could end up like, given the food he's fed. I gave my two cats really bad food until I read the back of the packet one day and threw the whole lot in the bin. I know better. Now.

Dogs get what they're given. But just like us, because we can eat whatever we like, which let's face it, is too much starchy, fatty, sugary and salty food, they are going on to develop diabetes, obesity, heart disease, cancer, skin rashes, tooth decay and loss, poor mobility, allergies and behavioural problems. And just like us, it's astonishingly easy to reduce the risk of all these diseases. By eating properly and

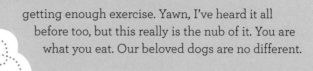

getting enough exercise. Yawn, I've heard it all before too, but this really is the nub of it. You are what you eat. Our beloved dogs are no different.

Three ways to feed your dog – which is best?

If you already have a dog you will know that, when it comes to food, everyone's an expert! In the blue corner we've got the supermarkets and large pet chains, backed up by multinationals, shouting loud and clear that their ready-made kibble is the best, that no one makes wet dog food like them, and the ingredients are second to none. In the red corner we've got devotees of raw food, gushing about the benefits of feeding dogs uncooked chicken wings and the size of their dogs' stools (teeny tiny) as a result of their dogs' ability to 'utilise' every scrap of said wing. Like having a child, having a dog is a very emotional thing and we take other people's opinions to heart. We want to make sure we're doing right by our four-legged friends, opening ourselves up to a lifetime of guilt and easy commercial persuasion.

I watched a TV programme on life in a zoo recently. I'd never considered what all the different animals ate on a daily basis before or what a job that must be for whoever managed the zoo's kitchen. Turns out the zoo has a full-time nutritionist employed to look after the welfare of their furry, feathery, leathery charges and he must take everything about their lives into account before working out what to feed them. Species, activity levels, age, boredom, etc are all considered before recipes, methods and timetables for feeding are made up for each animal. The nutritionist made a really interesting point that's stuck with me. He said, 'These animals are in such good condition because of what we feed them. If we were in there and they were out here and could eat all they like we'd be the ones in amazing shape. They (pointing to a honed-to-perfection group of tigers) would be fat because they could eat what they wanted. They're not programmed any differently from us.'

Wow. This could be the new craze – the 'Zoo Diet'. Lock me up and hide the key for six months. Feed me what I need, only when

I need it, and let me lounge about on a rock the rest of the day picking my feet, only moving occasionally to sidle up to a group of unsuspecting visitors and show them my backside, just like a chimpanzee. 'Does my bum look big in this? Oh no, I forgot, I've lost two stone!'

It's different for Charlie Average though. He will eat whatever I put in front of him. So I want to give him the best food I can afford to put in his dish. But how do I know what the best food is? I hear you ask.

Well, read on and I'll tell you. Basically, when it comes to feeding your dog, there are three main schools of thought: commercial dog food, home-cooked dog food and raw dog food. Which one you choose will depend on your particular circumstances, preferences and those of your dog. But by the time I'm done, I assure you, you'll be able to sniff out great dog food at a hundred yards. You will know the difference between a carrot and derivatives of vegetable origin and you'll regard most pet food marketing as laughable hype. The staff at PetsPetsPets will know not to try it on with you!

A BIT OF USEFUL BACKGROUND ON CANINE NUTRITION BEFORE WE START...

WHAT A DOG LOOKS FOR IN DOG FOOD

Your dog makes most of his eating decisions based upon his epic sense of smell. To put it into a human context, dogs have around 300 million olfactory receptors compared to our 40 million, roughly speaking. If we can smell a teaspoon of sugar in a glass of water, a dog could detect it in what it would take to fill two Olympic swimming pools. If you turn that into sight, where we can see well at a few hundred yards a dog would be able to see just at well at a few thousand miles. Their sense of smell is that powerful.

THE COLOUR OF DOG FOOD

We eat with our senses of sight and smell as well as taste, whereas dogs don't really get any value out of brightly coloured food because, while not actually colourblind, they don't see in the same way as we do. Colours are muted; dogs have more greys on their spectrum than humans so they're not swayed by colour. Brightly coloured packaging and kibble is there purely for our benefit. If your dog could wander the supermarket aisles unhindered, a lack of colour wouldn't be a deal-breaker.

DOG DIGESTION

A dog's digestion is somewhat different from our own. For starters it's much more acidic, which is why she generally gets away with snaffling two-day-old discarded pizza found in that bush over there, without picking up a dose of salmonella.

DOGS DON'T 'DO' DAIRY

By the time they are a year old dogs are lactose-intolerant. Cheese is fine in small amounts as the lactose is mostly extracted in the whey during processing – but best avoid milk, yoghurt and cream, because too much fat is very bad for a dog's liver. Eggs, on the other hand, are a good source of essential fatty acids.

WET FOOD VERSUS DRY FOOD

It doesn't matter if you feed dry kibble or wet food; it's a personal preference – that should be the dog's one really, not ours. Wet food contains more water, of course, but a good one will also contain far less cereal.

WHAT DOES A DOG NEED TO EAT WELL?

In simple terms, a dog needs a mix of good proteins, carbohydrates, fats, oils, vegetables and minerals. Pretty much in that order. After that it's trial and error to find out which food works best for your dog. For example, a working dog will need far more calories and carbs than a dog who only gets a couple of walks a day. A dog living outside will need more fat in winter, which could kill a dog with pancreatitis. Whether you choose prepared food, cook it yourself or feed raw, the balance of these food groups is essential for good health – your dog's energy, bones, digestion, coat condition and immunity.

'Can we have sausages? Pleeeasse!'

Commercial dog food

Commercial dog food is going to suit a lot of people, particularly those who don't have time to cook and don't have the freezer space for raw food. But knowing exactly which commercially produced dog food to go for is not so easy. Many people choose their dog food on price, either grabbing the cheapest and hoping for the best, or buying the most expensive on the grounds that you pay for what you get. Then there are debates about wet and dry. Questions about lifestage foods. Is it vital to get the right food for your dog's age, or is that just another marketing trick?

Commercial pet food must by law meet the minimum nutritional standards, as laid down by the European Pet Food Industry Federation (FEDIAF). But they are just that: minimum standards. So on the one hand you could say, feed a dog a complete food and you're good to go. On the other, all commercial dog foods are not created equal. Ingredient quality varies substantially, and you have to be an expert label reader, though even if you are, it doesn't mean you will know what's in it because food can be labelled in two ways, just to confuse you even more, hiding all sorts of ingredients. Your dog can live a good life on a complete, prepared dog food, whether it comes out of a packet, a tin or a pouch. It just depends on the quality of the ingredients.

The secrets of the pet food industry

The pet product market is big business in the UK – worth over £2bn annually. Five companies, Mars, Nestlé Purina, IAMS, Hills and Royal Canin, dominate the marketplace with over 90% share. Most household brands are owned by these five companies, which wield massive buying power for the raw materials and can more easily absorb supermarket tactics to get you in the door with Buy One Get One Free (BOGOFs) and other special offers. The economies of scale enjoyed by these big producers certainly assure you a level of quality, as well as consistency and security of supply.

However, the fact we buy the vast majority of our pet food and treats from the supermarket is a great shame, because, with the exception of one or two brands, better-value, healthier pet food can be bought online and in pet shops.

Super-premium brands

Prepared pet food has undergone something of a renaissance in the past few years. The increasing humanisation of pets – our dogs and cats are treated more like family members than ever now – means we want to give our dogs something resembling what we eat ourselves. Hence the growth in what the pet industry terms super-premium brands – with the focus on foods labelled Organic, Natural and Holistic. At the same time, pet owners have become increasingly demanding as consumers, in the wake of a series of food scares: BSE, foot and mouth, melamine poisoning and salmonella contamination.

The development of super-premium pet foods has been further fuelled by the fact that the pet food market has become so saturated by brands that producers find it increasingly hard to stand out from the crowd. Rising labour, energy and ingredient costs have meant it is very difficult to make money on economy foods, so many companies have developed high-end lines and have seen rapid growth.

But exactly how high-end are they? Like any big new thing, there are better and worse examples. What you should know, though, is that in processing terms these upmarket brands are very similar to most economy foods. New products are designed to fit into the current processing methods, not the other way around. It's just too expensive to develop new manufacturing processes to retain more of a food's original nutritional value, and why would you when you can add it later?

What's in commercial dog food?

The key ingredients of any commercially produced dog food can be broken down into the categories of protein, fat, carbohydrate, fibre, mineral and additive/nutraceuticals.

Common protein sources are meat meals – a 'meal' is animal flesh that's been dehydrated to be reconstituted when made into food – a mixture of beef, lamb, pork, poultry (chicken, turkey, duck, or a blend) and fish (generally a mix of ocean-caught fish).

Individual species meals are also available, such as salmon, lamb, chicken, etc. Other common protein sources are vegetable-based, such as potato, pea, soya, yeast and maize gluten. Generally, dogs and cats digest meat proteins better than vegetable, and the amino acid balance is more suitable. Excess amino acids have to be excreted and put pressure on the liver and kidneys.

Fat sources are also usually either animal- or vegetable-based. Animal-fat sources include chicken, poultry, pork and fish. Vegetable sources are usually either soya or sunflower.

Carbs are of course usually vegetable-based, and include cereals such as wheat, maize, rice and barley, but also tubers and pulses such as potato, tapioca, cassava and pea.

Fibres are often supplied in the form of sugar-beet pulp or alfalfa (grass), and also grain by-products such as rice hulls and wheatfeed (wheat husks) in some more economical foods.

Minerals are sometimes added to balance the major mineral content (calcium, phosphorus, sodium, etc). A pre-blended mixture of approximately 12 vitamins and 6 trace minerals are added to ensure the minimum nutritional requirements are met.

How is pet food produced?

Pet food is generally prepared by a process known as extrusion. If it's a dry kibble the ingredients are mixed together, then cooked using steam at around 140oC. The mixture is then pushed through a tube, coming out the other end as dry kibble or biscuits. Fat and digest are added at this point, but the vast majority of the nutrients are added at the start of the process. A wet food will be sealed and cooked in a can, pouch or tray so it's not exposed to bacteria after cooking.

Baking is another cooking process. Like extrusion, it is primarily designed to cook starch so is done at high temperatures. There is no evidence to suggest that it is nutritionally superior.

And then there is air-drying – which can reduce the loss of naturally present nutrients. However, air-drying can introduce its own challenges, such as bacterial spoilage and mould growth, if not done properly.

Some companies use a significant amount of poetic licence in describing their ingredients, such as 'air-dried chicken protein' to describe chicken meat meal. It is misleading and not strictly legal. Drying anything usually involves the use of air, even if it is blasted through a hot oven in an industrial site in China, but 'air-dried' gives the impression that it is hung out in the midday sun on some Mediterranean island!

How to read the label

Doing research for this book I read a lot of pet food labels, and I mean a lot! They don't make it easy for you to choose the best food. The hyperbole on the front is practically meaningless, the colours are there for you, not the dog, and a high price is not necessarily an indicator of high quality.

The other day I was browsing in the pet food aisle in the supermarket and came across a dry dog food containing over 60% cereal – meat was the third ingredient on the label; furthermore, this food garnered a fair bit of its protein from vegetable fibres. I'm failing to see how that's a good thing.

Go to the kitchen cupboard and get your current packet, pouch or can down and take a good look at what you bought. Ask yourself: what made you buy this brand? Word of mouth? Did the vet tell you to feed it because it was 'bland' and shouldn't cause any issues? Was it super-expensive? Does it have the kind of packaging design to make it look as if it's been lovingly hand-baked by the ladies at the WI?

Right, take a look at the front of the packet. Is there a photo of a cute, vital and energetic dog 'enjoying life to the full' in a sunny meadow on the front? I bet it says something like 'food your dog will love you for' and 'using only natural ingredients', 'no artificial additives' etc. And this may well be the case. But that's all hype and sales pitch. The real story is on the back. That's where you find what you're looking for. The list of ingredients.

So, let's not believe the hype, let's learn to read a label. What you need to be able to do is translate and understand that ingredients list. When you can do that, when you know what those ingredients mean and how they apply to your dog and his diet, you will have the power to sally forth into your local or online pet shop (because you'll never want to get your food anywhere else in future) and demand the best food out there, because you will know what you're looking for. No more 'various sugars' for you, oh no!

The mysterious language of ingredients lists

Food labelling laws state that 'all ingredients must be listed in order of weight, with the main ingredient listed first'. Rabbit, chicken, peas, swede, carrots, cranberry, seaweed, for example. You also have to show the percentage of an ingredient if it is 'highlighted by the labelling or a picture on a package'. So 'chicken and turkey casserole' on the front of the label should read chicken 45%, turkey 15% on the ingredients list.

Beyond that, food can be listed on labels in two ways – either as a single ingredient, e.g. 'chicken', or as a category, e.g. 'meat and animal derivatives'. If you list an ingredient as chicken then it can only be the flesh and a little bone. It cannot be tendon or skin, for example. The same goes for 'chicken meal', which may be reconstituted, but which must once have been chicken flesh.

If the label states 'meat and animal derivatives (min 4% chicken)' and the meat content is 26% overall, then you won't know what the remaining 22% is. It can be beef, pork, lamb or a combination of all three. The term 'meat and animal derivatives' allows pet food producers to use the flesh and 'all products and derivatives of the processing of the carcass or parts of the carcass' over which you have no control. They list ingredients this way because it gives them more flexibility and enables them to buy the cheapest ingredients at any given moment. If they're getting pork £1 a tonne cheaper than beef that week, they're going to use it. Margins are tight.

It's no different for cereals or vegetables. If the label states 'rice', it must be rice, not rice husks. The same goes for 'wheat': it cannot be wheat husks. If, however, the label simply states 'cereals' as a category, the food can contain wheat, maize, rice, wheat gluten and wheatfeed (husks) in any combination. No good if you're trying to keep your dog off wheat.

Vegetables will either read 'carrot, broccoli, pea', in which case they must be just that and not a by-product such as the husk or 'derivatives of vegetable

origin', which can be a mixture of any vegetables and their by-products (i.e. what's left after the good stuff's been syphoned off for use in something else). So, again, you won't know what you're getting.

The category 'various sugars', by the way, means 'all types of sugar', literally.

As I say, category labelling can cause problems for the owner whose dog has difficulty digesting certain ingredients. Many dogs don't get on well with beef, for example, and research is starting to show that dogs exposed to the same protein repeatedly over years could develop an intolerance to it. The only way you can control the ingredients your dog eats is by selecting food that lists ingredients individually.

Understanding what it says on the tin...

 DRY FOOD

Typical ingredients in a good food

	Why
Chicken 61% (from dried chicken)	If it says chicken it can only be chicken flesh. It's the first ingredient and 61%
Chicken mince 10.5%	More chicken making it 71.5%
Peas 8%	Peas!
Potato starch 6%	Another carb making it a 14% carb total so far
Poultry oil 2.5%	A good oil. You know it must come from poultry
Lamb 5%	More meat
Beet pulp	A good source of fibre
Poultry gravy & whole egg	All this before we get to the minerals, vitamins and herbs

Typical ingredients in a shocking food

	Why
Cereals	You don't know which cereals are included, the quality of them, and they should NEVER be first on the list
Meat and animal derivatives (26 % meat, 4% beef)	Only 4% is beef, the rest can be any meat, so if your dog has an intolerance you don't know what to
Various sugars	Not necessary in dog food
Vegetable protein extracts	Protein should be meat-based as much as possible as it's easier for a dog to digest and better for the liver and kidneys
Oils and fats	Which oils and fats? By-products from the ice cream industry or decent healthy stuff?
Minerals	OK but in what quantity?

WET FOOD

Typical ingredients in a good food

	Why
Lamb 65%	It's got to be just lamb flesh. Easily digestible meat
Rice 10%	Great protein-to-carb ratio
Vegetables 7%	Just veg. Can't be derivatives
Ground bone	A great source of calcium
Seaweed meal	Great B vitamins

Typical ingredients in a shocking food

	Why
Meat and animal derivatives (42%, including 4% chicken)	So if it's 4% chicken what's the other 38% made up of?
Cereals	Which carbs are these? No good if your dog is wheat-intolerant
Oils and fats (including 1% sunflower oil),	What type of oils and fats and where from?
Derivatives of vegetable origin (including 0.8% dried sugar beet pulp),	So no whole veg. Granted, beet pulp is a good source of fibre
Minerals	Which minerals?
Vegetable protein extracts	Not as digestible to dogs as animal protein. And so far down the list as to be pointless

TREATS

Great treat — meat or fish	Why
Sardines 70%	Lots of fish, will be very smelly to dogs. They won't need a lot of this.
Oats	Single carb, not 'cereals'
Herbs	Herbs

Great treat — vegetable	Why
Sweet potato 100%	Good source of slow release carbs. Good source of vitamin A and C too.

Shocking treat	Why
Cereals	Carbohydrate is the first ingredient. Undefined at that so they don't even have to be whole cereals
Minerals	If this is the second ingredient you know the carbs make up the vast majority of this dog treat
Meat and animal derivatives	Only added for flavour it's so far down the list
Derivatives of vegetable origin	Poor fibre source
Oils and fats	From where?

In summary:

Brands are very good at employing smoke and mirrors to hide cheap ingredients. To ensure you're getting a higher-quality food keep these key tips in mind when scanning a label.

Choose a food that lists ingredients singly, not as a group.

The first ingredients should always be meat or fish.

Make sure they're not swiftly followed by two or more carbohydrate sources, such as rice, potato starch and maize, otherwise the total carbohydrate can account for more than the protein, even though this is listed first.

Avoid food with added colours.

Avoid food listing sugars or added sugars.
.
If ingredients such as fruit, vegetables, herbs and supplements occur further down the list than 'minerals' they are generally being included purely for marketing and will be insufficient to be effective.

'Paw = treat.
Honest'

NUTRACEUTICALS

These are the supposedly magic ingredients that we find in human foods: supplements that promise to lower cholesterol, or probiotic drinks that claim to balance our gut flora. They are now a big thing in commercially produced dog food.

As a human, I'm not convinced. I eat a varied diet. I don't think probiotic drinks contain enough of the active ingredient to do any good in the first place, plus many of them also contain a fair bit of added sugar.

It's not quite the same for dogs, though. If they're on the same food, day in day out, adding a good amount of probiotic will stop them farting, and a decent helping of valerian will give them a better night's sleep. I think the rule of thumb should be: if you're wanting to add some benefit to her diet then a good food or treat with added nutraceutical value is fine, just make sure the ingredients are sound – i.e. that they're added in sufficient quantities and are of good quality.

Check how far down the list nutraceuticals come on the label. Remember: ingredients are listed by the greatest amount included in food first – chicken 26%, barley 12%, salmon oil 2%, etc. Nutraceuticals should come as an ingredient in their own right – salmon oil = omega 3 – or as a supplement – glucosamine. And in either case they should certainly be listed above any minerals on the ingredients list to stand a chance of being any use to your dog.

If you're unsure, talk to the producers and ask their advice. If they're not forthcoming, don't buy it.

READ THIS:
Brown rice 67% (carbs), chicken meal 20%, oats (more carbs), peas (even more carbs!), chicken oil, sunflower oil and seaweed. That's not what I want to be feeding my dog.

With that in mind...

Look at the label again and ask yourself this: 'If I walk into the supermarket right now, will I be able to buy this list of ingredients, as stand-alone products, more or less?' If the answer is yes – chicken, rice, carrots, peas, ground bone – it's more than likely a great dog food. If the answer is no – meat and animal derivatives, derivatives of vegetable origin, cereals and hydrolysed animal proteins – it's not the best.

Don't be fooled by the term 'natural' on the packaging. It indicates that the components have not been bleached, oxidised or chemically treated, but it does not tell you anything about the actual quality of the food. 'Wheatfeed', i.e. the husk of the wheat, can be described as 'natural' but it has minimal nutritional value for your dog.

And don't be fooled into thinking that because a food is expensive or labelled as a super-premium brand it's going to have a great balance of protein to carbs. I just perused the site of a well-known brand that prides itself on its ingredients. They may well be exceptional quality but one food was nearly 70% carbohydrate!

The affordability factor

However you cut it, the pet food market is driven by us, the customers. If we want to keep the cost of feeding Fido down, and prices of raw materials and energy continue to rise, ultimately the things that have to give are ingredients and recipe quality.

The quantity of meat meals and cereals that companies like Mars and Nestlé Purina consume is vast, and it is not always possible for them to obtain consistent quality at a consistent price. This means three things: they compromise on quality, they put the price up or they amend the recipe (or a combination of all three).

The good thing about the premium foods is that they usually declare ingredients individually, so there's less scope for recipe adaptation. But then you are paying more for them.

The truth is that until we're happy to pay a higher price, more often, for better food, the status quo will prevail. I wouldn't say that the pet food industry has been complicit in harming the health of pets through greed or negligence, but the industry that has developed probably isn't sustainable in the future. Nobody wants to make the first move and put the price of standard dog foods up by 50%, which is what probably needs to happen to get back to better nutrition.

The pros of commercial dog food:

Easy to budget: you know how much it's costing to feed your dog

Quick and easy to prepare

Highly regulated: it should be safe and not pose any health problems

Consistent quality: you know your dog will eat it and you're not going to be throwing it away

There are some very good prepared dog foods on the market these days

Dry food keeps well, and you don't need fridge space for it

Complete food is simple: you don't have to worry about supplements

The cons of commercial dog food

You have no control over the quality of ingredients

Dry foods can contain more carbohydrates than proteins

Labelling food using categories makes it hard to know precisely what ingredients you're getting

Like any other food, it's going to be trial and error while you find a food that works for your dog

Eating the same food over and over is more boring to a dog than watching cricket is to a right-thinking human. There, I said it

Should we buy British?

The 'made in the UK' label proudly displayed on pet food really does make a difference. This is borne out by the fact that many foreign pet food manufacturers still buy their super-premium foods from UK producers. This is due to three factors: the quality of meat meals and fats are higher in the UK than most other countries in the world owing to our moderate climate; the equipment is generally very modern and operators knowledgeable; and we generally adhere to the regulations and are seen as trustworthy.

An absence of recent pet food scares recently in the UK is one upside (if you can call it that) of the outbreaks of BSE, salmonella and foot and mouth we've suffered in the past 20 years. We have benefited from new regulation around traceability, movement of animals and accountability.

Should I even consider a 'lifestage food'?

We don't have them for old humans, so why do we need them for old dogs? Generally it is a marketing tool used to differentiate products and hence gain customer loyalty. However, as dogs have to obtain virtually all of their nutrients from one food, there is an argument for offering different foods. For example, we might take joint supplements in old age or drink more milk when young to provide extra calcium. The majority of pet owners do not want to supplement, so lifestage foods are an option.

AM I TOO LATE?

If you think it's a bit late in the day to change your dog's diet then think again. It's seldom too late and very easy to do.

Here's a true story. My osteopath likes to keep her Lhasa apso in her treatment room with her. P is 12 years old and has his own chair with a blanket to sit on from which he likes to watch a steady stream of patients getting kneaded, manipulated and generally put back together again.

About a year ago, poor P was diagnosed with a 'bellyful of cancer' after he'd stopped eating. The vet gave little P a couple of weeks at best. Now I don't know why it suddenly triggered a change in diet – I'd nagged her about

it often enough – but she took P off his famous-brand tinned food, and put him on Nature Diet – a wet food containing 65% chicken, rice, veg, ground bone and seaweed.

Now P is still with us, one year on, still looking across at me, while I sit in my underwear, thinking, 'Really love, you couldn't get it together to dress in matching bra and knickers today?' Now I hear the cynic in you saying, 'How can a change of diet do that?' Well, he still has cancer, but he's still here. He's eating well – he goes mad for food in a way he never did before, and can just about always make the stairs unaided (well, he is 12)!

A REASSURING STORY

In 2012, as part of a bid to raise money for Children in Need, I ate nothing but dog treats for two days (I was really choosy about what I ate, and very grumpy by the end of it, but I wasn't ill!). I should point out that they were produced in the UK and China. I can still taste that dried pig snout. As Mick Dundee succinctly put it in the 1981 film *Crocodile Dundee*, 'You can live on it but it tastes like s**t!'

Sitting
pretty

Home cooking for your dog

The second and by far the least controversial way to feed your dog is by cooking her meals.

The pros of home cooking are simple: you know precisely what's gone into your dog's dinner; it's simple to shop for; and it's a great way to use up leftovers too, as long as you're selective.

Here's a story (admittedly, a human one) about the value of home cooking. A few years ago I was working on a TV programme about food additives in human food, and one of the things we wanted to find out was 'are ready meals as healthy, nutritionally speaking, as home-made dishes?' In the programme we did a couple of things. The first was meal testing. I made a shepherd's pie – mince, onions, carrots, tomatoes and mashed potato made from scratch. That was pretty much it. Then I took a middle-of-the-road ready-meal shepherd's pie from each of the big supermarkets and sent the lot off to be tested for nutritional value at a well-known food research establishment.

Before they left, I turfed the contents of the plastic trays out into their own identical storage boxes (mixed them up a bit in there so they all looked pretty modged up), added my home-made version to another box and marked them A, B, C, D and E for anonymity.

Once at the lab, each serving of food was blended and a sample taken to be measured for protein, fat, carb, salt and sugar levels. Now the ingredients listed on the ready meals weren't at all obnoxious, and they were very clearly listed, but the results were phenomenal. The home-made version easily came out on top. Best protein levels, lowest sugar and salt levels and not bad in the fat stakes either. Simply by cooking at home you're getting better nutrition, because you can keep an eye on fat levels, quality of ingredients and temperatures. Your food is being cooked in a standard oven, not sealed in a tray to be heated until all bacteria are slain!

Secondly, we enlisted the help of a family of six – Mum, Dad and four kids – asking them to live an additive-free life for six weeks. These people were legends in our eyes, especially Mum, because literally all their food and drink had to be thought through. If there was an additive in it, they couldn't have it. Have a look in the fridge, in your cupboards, and really think about it for a moment. Shop-bought bread – nope! All made by hand from now on. No stabilisers, crumb-softening enzymes or added sugar for them. Rice, yes, fruit, veg, meat and fish, yes, but all without anything added to them. Biscuits? No. Fruit drinks? No. Sweets and chocolate? Definitely not. Cheese? Yes, but only proper cheese, not processed with added 'cheese food' or stabilisers. Bacon or other processed meats? Not allowed. Yoghurt? Hmmmm... natural only.

At the start, everyone in the family had a blood test. We tested them for cholesterol, blood sugar levels, vitamins C, B, D, iron levels, etc. At the end of the six weeks we took bloods again and those results were pretty great too. Cholesterol and blood sugar levels, all down. Vitamin levels, all up substantially, especially vitamin C. They had more energy and were sleeping better too.

That's why I cook my own meals and why we cook for the dogs. You can't blame food manufacturers. They're making food to make a profit, and it must be safe for us to eat. The only disadvantage of cooking for your dog is that it takes a bit of thought and forward-planning. (And we do have Nature Diet or similar on standby for those nights we forget, are on the move, or are not cooking for anyone, including ourselves.)

Dos and don'ts of cooking for your dog

 DO:

Keep ingredients simple

Cook in batches

Take advantage of supermarket offers and bulk buy, then freeze what you don't need

Ask your butcher or meat counter to order bones in for you if they don't already stock them

Avoid food loved by humans but poisonous to dogs

DON'T:

Assume that the dog can eat everything you can

Think that a dog can happily digest two-week-old food

Buy frozen, bargain-basement chickens, which will be padded out with sugar, salt and water

Food that is poisonous or dangerous to dogs

Chocolate — the darker it is the worse it is

Xylitol — found in human diet products and toothpaste

Alcohol

Onions

Raisins and grapes — no one knows why

Cooked bones — will splinter

Small bones — choking hazard - go for something they can barely get their mouth round, with a bit of meat on

Avocados — contain a fungicidal toxin called persin

Caffeine — coffee, tea, soft drinks

Milk/yoghurt/cream — contain lactose, and will upset stomach

Macadamia nuts

Sweets and chewing gum — contain xylitol

Fat trimmings from meat — pancreatitis

Soft fruit stones in peaches, plums, cherries — can cause inflammation of the gut

Salt and sugar

Raw potatoes

Pips and seeds — toxic if enough eaten

Rhubarb

Food that is safe and beneficial for dogs

Lean meat and fish

Apples, oranges, bananas and watermelon – remove the seeds first

Carrots

Broccoli

Green beans

Cucumber

Courgettes

Plain rice

Pumpkin

Sweet potatoes

Porridge oats

Cooked potatoes

Brewer's yeast

How I do it

I cook once a week, on average. I'll get whatever looks good or is on offer, preferably both, then cook rice with the meat, a little garlic and some raw veg (carrots, broccoli, sprouts, whatever's about) and stick it in the oven. When it's cool it's divided up into portions for the week. Some goes in the dogs, some in the fridge and the rest into the freezer.

They all get fed twice a day. Ronnie won't eat in front of you, so he takes each mouthful of food to the back door where we can't see him eating.

Funny little thing. He is an out-and-out carnivore who will lick gravy off a pea and leave the pea on the side. BB was fed on tinned (not good tinned) food until we got her, so will eat anything you put in front of her. When we first got Nikita she just inhaled her food, but now she knows she gets fed every night she's slowed right down. She'll eat veg that's well mixed in with the meat, she doesn't like fish, but she does like the cat's food and will eat that too if she can get away with it.

That's pretty much it. They get a raw egg once in a while, raw bones, chopped veg for BB and the odd treat. When you consider that Ronnie has never had a weight problem and BB was fat when we got her but now doesn't have a pick on her, we know it's good. Nikita is a stable weight, too, and her breath has greatly improved since I changed her over to home cooked. Raw did not agree with her; it was too rich, resulting in epic dog breath. Our dogs are energetic, but not crazy, and they're in great shape.

The key here is not to feed too much of the same food all the time. Mix it up. Plain rice is fine but you don't want too much. Garlic is OK, but again, only a little (onions are poisonous for dogs, but garlic is fine in moderation, even though they're from the same family). Sweet potato is a great source of fibre, complex carbs and vitamins A and D, but it's very starchy, so not too much. Eggs need be free range, not battery. Variety + balance = a healthy dog.

to her 'restaurant eyes'. She can even make herself tear up if she's not getting her own way.

Leftovers the dog can eat

Meat – fat and skin removed

Fish – without bones

Vegetables – cooked plainly without anything added

Potatoes – if you've got a bit of mash left over, or a boiled potato, great. Stay clear of anything Dauphinoise-like, or chips!

Leftovers the dog can't eat

Fatty meat or fatty foods in general – these can easily cause pancreatitis in dogs

Foods to which you've added salt and pepper – take any seasoned skin off meat

Stay away from stews and casseroles for the same reasons – fat, salt, Worcestershire sauce, red wine, garlic, onions – bad for dogs, especially in the quantities we cook them in

Gravy – even home-made will have salt added, or a stock cube, and if it's out of a jar then definitely no

Fast food

The leftovers debate

To feed or not to feed your dog leftovers, that is the question. Some will say absolutely not; but if you're going to, keep to the really simple stuff and make them just an occasional treat. Don't give leftovers to the dog from the table, especially if she's a keen beggar; put them in her bowl.

Nikita will beg at the drop of a hat and, being an ex-street dog, she's got that look nailed! No one is immune

10 TOP DOGS' DINNERS

Ingredient weights in these recipes are approximate so don't stress about getting it spot on. If you're short of a carrot, substitute something else you have in which is safe for dogs. This isn't Masterchef: there won't be any long pauses or steely-eyed stares, and your dog won't be critiquing your use of flavours and textures. She will be too busy stuffing her face.

You might want to give finished dishes a rough mash with a potato masher if you need to disguise the veg. Serve some to your dog warm (not hot), put some in the fridge for use over the next couple of days and freeze the rest.

Have a bag of frozen veg in the freezer. It's a really fast way of getting veg into their food. Because it's frozen it will mash up quite well when cooked, making it easier to mix into the rest of their food.

I also keep vegetable peelings – carrots, broccoli, cabbage and sprouts mostly – which I then steam in the microwave and blitz in a small food processor. It keeps in the fridge for a few days and I add it to their food each day. Free food!

I don't add salt and pepper or use any human gravy or stock cubes in my recipes because they are mostly salt themselves. Dogs have a phenomenal sense of taste and too much salt is really bad for their kidneys.

Pork and Potato Stew

Pork belly is a cheap but highly nutritious cut of meat. It can be pretty fatty, though, so I cut some of it off; and then, when it's cooked and cooled, I skim more fat off the top and discard it.

1kg pork belly
200g liver
200g sweet potato
1 clove of garlic, chopped
1 bag of frozen chopped spinach
A handful of parsley, chopped
100g rice

Cut your pork belly, liver and sweet potato into 3cm-ish chunks and put them in an ovenproof dish or pan. Add the bag of frozen spinach, chopped garlic, the uncooked rice and cover with water.

Cover the dish and put it in the oven at 160°C, 325°F or Gas 3 until it's all cooked – the sweet potato is soft, the rice and pork tender. Mix in the parsley and give it another five minutes. Keep an eye on the water and top up as necessary as the cooking rice absorbs it.

Chicken and Vegetable Gluten-free Stew

Dead easy to make, takes five minutes to put together.

1 tray (approximately 850g) of fresh chicken thighs and drumsticks
A couple of large carrots, chopped
1 head of broccoli including the stalk, chopped, or a bag of frozen broccoli
A good handful of spring greens, chopped
A glug of vegetable oil

Mix the whole lot together in an oven-proof dish with a lid, cover with water and bake in the oven at 160°C, 325°F or Gas 3 until it's all cooked.

Allow it to cool, then pick the meat from the bones. Make sure you trawl for any bones left behind, especially the really thin ones, and throw them away, along with the chicken skin.

Give it a light mash to bind it all together and serve.

Skin & Bones

A hearty recipe for when you want to put some meat on your skinny dog. If she's lost weight due to illness, or you just picked up a scrawny stray from the rescue centre, this is a good dinner.

1kg minced beef, pork or lamb
250g giblets (heart, neck, liver, etc. Ask the butcher)
100g white or brown rice, or wholemeal pasta
450g mixed vegetables – I would buy a bag of frozen cauliflower, carrots and broccoli for this
2 large eggs, hardboiled and chopped
A large handful of parsley, chopped
Vegetable oil

Heat up the vegetable oil in a large, heavy-bottomed pan. Brown the mince and giblets. Add the frozen veg and the rice or pasta, cover with water, put the lid on and turn down to a simmer.

Check the water level after a few minutes and add more if it looks like the mixture is drying out. When the rice is cooked and there's a bit of liquid left, it's done. Add the chopped hardboiled eggs and parsley, give it a stir and serve. When serving over the next couple of days I'd add a good omega oil blend too.

A wholesome supper for hungry dogs

Fish Friday

An easy-peasy fish recipe – basically fish pie for dogs.

2 large potatoes, peeled
and chopped
100g frozen peas
1 large tin of salmon
1 tin of tuna in spring
water, drained
300g cooked white fish – I
use frozen coley portions,
defrosted and steamed
A large handful of parsley,
chopped
2 large eggs, hardboiled

Peel, chop and boil the potatoes in unsalted water. Mash them up. Don't worry about adding milk or butter as most dogs are lactose-intolerant by the age of one. While the potatoes are boiling, take the opportunity to cook the frozen peas too.

In a large bowl, mix the salmon, tuna and cooked white fish together. Add the chopped egg and chopped parsley and mix thoroughly. Then add the mashed potatoes and peas and mix again.

It should be more fish than potato at the end of it. Portion it up and serve.

Fish & Chips

Wot, no
ketchup?

Picnic Muffins (yes, really)

Take a sandwich for yourself and these for your dog and doggy friends.

800g cooked lentils – that's two tins, just drain and rinse before using
2 cucumbers, roughly chopped
a bag of frozen chopped spinach or a couple of
1 bag fresh spinach, chopped up
1kg minced lamb, chicken or pork

Mix the lentils, cucumbers and spinach either by hand or preferably in a food processor until you've got a good paste. Add to the minced meat and mix it all together.

Now portion it up into roughly golf-ball-sized portions, rolling them into shape with your hands.

Put them on a greased baking tray and cook at 160°C, 325°F or Gas 3 until done, around 15 minutes.

Serve them warm or store in an airtight container in the fridge or freezer. I pack a few frozen muffins into my backpack so they've defrosted when the dog gets them a few hours later.

Turkey, Pear Mash and Oat Muffins

2 large pears
1kg lean turkey mince
(you can really use any
lean minced meat you
like)
125g porridge oats
1 large courgette, finely
chopped
2 large eggs (reserve the
shells)
2 tbsp vegetable oil

Core your pears, chop them up and put them in a pan with 100ml water. Bring to the boil then simmer until they're soft enough to mash with a fork. Don't add any sugar – there's enough in the pears themselves. You want to end up with a nice runny mix so add more water if necessary.

Put the turkey mince, courgette, porridge oats, pear mash, eggs and vegetable oil in a large bowl and mix well.

Take to the eggshells with a rolling pin or a hand-blender and don't stop until they're a fine powder. Now tip them into the bowl too and mix everything together.

Roll the mixture into balls – the size you settle on is for you and the dog to work out between you! Bake on a greased baking tray at 200°C 400°F or Gas 6 for 20 minutes. Turf out onto a wire rack, and allow to cool.

Christmas Dinner for Dogs

Did you know that if we wanted to walk off the average Christmas lunch we would have to march, non-stop, for 36 hours? Apparently. We really go to town on the high-fat, high-salt options on Christmas Day. So this is a low-fat, no-salt, alternative festive treat for your dog. Make it in advance to save yourself a job on the day.

100g minced turkey
50g cooked rice
1 small carrot, grated
A couple of Brussels sprouts, finely chopped
Vegetable oil

Heat the oil in a small frying pan. Add the mince and cook through. Stir in the rice, grated carrot and sprouts. Put a lid on the pan and let it steam for a few minutes, allowing the rice to soak up the meat juices and the vegetables to soften. When it's all thoroughly cooked and heated through, remove from the heat and allow to cool right down before serving.

Merry Christmas, pooch!

Salmon & Vegetable Fishcakes

A clean and simple meal. Easy for a recovering dog to digest.

200g fresh salmon fillet
150g mixed vegetables
100g mashed potato
(no butter, salt or milk
added)

Steam the salmon fillet until cooked then flake it into a bowl.

Steam your mixed vegetables – carrot, broccoli, green beans, for instance – and add to the salmon, along with the potato. Mix the lot together until it's all good and blended.

Serve warm. Any leftovers can be kept in the fridge for a couple of days.

Doggie Con Carne

Dogs need protein, they also need fibre, so if you're wanting to get both into them, try adding beans to their meals. This recipe does it all.

1 tbsp vegetable oil
1kg lean beef mince
1 tin kidney beans, drained
and rinsed
1 really big carrot
1 big squeeze of tomato
purée

Heat the oil in a large pan and brown the mince. Tip the tin of beans into the pan, chop the carrot and add that too. Squeeze the tomato purée on top, add 500ml water and give it a good stir. Cover and simmer for 20 minutes. Allow to cool and serve. Leftovers can be stored in the fridge for a couple of days and the rest frozen.

Chicken Salad

A good one for hot days. Cottage cheese is pretty digestible as most of the lactose is removed in the making.

1 chicken leg, roasted and left to cool
1 small tub of cottage cheese (full fat)
1 carrot, grated
A handful of green beans
A handful of parsley, chopped
A glug of good omega oil (I like Yumega Plus)

Pick the cold meat off the chicken leg and discard the skin and bones. Chop the meat up roughly, put it in a bowl and mix together with the cottage cheese. Add the grated carrot. Steam the green beans, run them under cold water, then chop them and add them to the mixture, along with the parsley and oil. Mix the lot together and serve.

Your dog says thank you.

🐾 DOG TREATS 🐾

There's more at the end of this chapter on treats – how to choose a good one if you're buying them in, and how to give them wisely. But, if you want to go homemade, here are some great tasty recipe ideas...

Chicken Pupsicles (or Soup)

Summer favourite

When the weather starts to perk up I make these, in anticipation of the hot days ahead, and freeze them in ice cube trays. Because it's a blended recipe and you can't detect the veg my cats love them too. Remember which are the chicken cubes and which are real ice. They do nothing for a gin and tonic.

A tray of fresh chicken thighs and drumsticks
A small bag of frozen vegetables

You can use a whole chicken for this recipe. I just prefer pieces because they take a lot less time to cook through than a whole bird. This also works well as a warm soup in winter.

Put the chicken pieces and vegetables in a heavy-bottomed pan and cover with water. Bring to the boil then turn down to a simmer for around 20 minutes, or until everything is cooked through. Turn off the heat and leave to cool.

Take the meat off the bones and discard them along with the skin, then blend everything together – meat, veg and cooking water – either in a food processor or with a hand blender. If the resulting mix is a little too gloopy, add some cold water to thin it a little. Pour it into ice cube trays and freeze. Dole out a few cubes on a hot day to keep your dog cool and entertained.

Veggie Seedy Patties

These are a wheat-free treat containing lots of good fibre. Quite calorie dense so definitely a 'treat'.

50g sunflower seeds
250g oat flour
1 tbsp ground flaxseed
5 tbsp olive oil
1 tsp fresh parsley, finely chopped
125ml water

Preheat the oven to 180°C, 350°F or Gas 4. Chop up the sunflower seeds with a knife or stick them in the food processor. Put them in a bowl with the rest of the ingredients and mix together until you've got a good dough. Break the dough off into pieces about the size of a golf ball (about 25g per piece) and mash each one down lightly with a fork. Put these rough patties on a greased baking tray and bake for 30-40 minutes. Cool on a wire rack. they can be stored in an airtight container or in the fridge for up to a week.

Jerky

Jerky for humans and rawhide for pets is often treated with preservatives. Making your own is a good option if you've got the time and the inclination.

2 chicken breasts
2 large sweet potatoes

Preheat the oven to 100°C 200°F Gas 1. Remove any fat from the chicken, peel the sweet potato and slice them both into 5mm-thick strips. Lie them on a lightly greased baking sheet (I use good greaseproof paper for this) and bake them for a couple of hours. The strips should be hard and dry, not soft. The aim is to get as much moisture out of them as possible so they don't spoil. Leave them to cool on a wire rack, then store them for up to two weeks.

Apple and Cheese Treats

I don't know any dog who doesn't like cheese, especially hard cheese. A good Cheddar always goes down well, in very small amounts, of course. So try these out. The combination of the sweetness of the apple and the savouriness of the cheese means they won't hang about for long.

400g oat flour
100g porridge oats
150g mature Cheddar, grated
150g apple
2 tbsp vegetable oil

Preheat the oven to 180°C, 350°F gas 4. Chop the apple, remove the core and cook it with a little water in a small pan. When it's nice and soft, set it aside to cool.

Mix the stewed apple with all the other ingredients, then add enough water to bind the mixture together to form a dough (about 150ml). On a floured surface, roll the dough out to about 1cm thick and cut into biscuits – how big will depend on the size of dog they're intended for.

Lay them on a lined baking sheet and bake until they're golden brown. Turn off the oven and leave them to cool down, dry out a little more and harden. When the oven is cold take the biscuits out and store them in an airtight container.

Banana and Peanut Butter Treats

1 banana
200g oat flour
A small handful of fresh parsley
A small handful of fresh mint
3 tbsp peanut butter (the kind with no added salt or sugar)
1 egg, beaten

Preheat the oven to 150°C, 300°F or gas 2. In a large bowl mash up the banana, then add the flour, parsley, mint, peanut butter and egg and mix until they're all combined. If the dough is a bit dry, add a tbsp of water to help it bind. Put the mixture in the fridge for 20 minutes to cool and firm up.

Roll the mixture into golf-ball-sized treats. Transfer them to a greased (or grease-proof-papered) baking sheet and flatten each one slightly. Bake for 40-45 minutes. These will keep for a couple of weeks in an airtight container in the fridge.

Coconut and Brewer's Yeast Treats

Coconut oil is one of those super-foods we don't get enough of. Lots of good fat and antibacterial properties make this an essential ingredient in everyone's diet. Brewer's yeast is a good source of B vitamins.

400g oat flour
100g brewers yeast
40ml coconut oil
300ml home-made chicken stock or water

Preheat the oven to 200°C, 400°F or Gas 6. Mix the flour and brewer's yeast together then add the coconut oil and mix again. Add the stock or water to the mixture and combine well until you have a dough. Adjust the liquid as necessary to get the right consistency. Roll the dough out to 5mm thick on a floured surface and cut into biscuits using your cutter of choice. Place them on a greased and lined baking tray and bake for 20 minutes. Turn the oven off to let them crisp up in the oven.

Liver Cake

By far and away the easiest, tastiest and most adored treat you can make for your dog. The downside is it does smell out the kitchen, so make it on a day when you can throw open all the doors and windows.

250g liver
125g oat flour
2 large eggs
2 cloves of garlic

Preheat the oven to 180°C, 350°F or Gas 4. Line a greased cake tin or tray with greaseproof paper. Roughly chop the liver and whizz it in a food processor or blender. Add the flour, eggs and garlic to the liquidised liver and whizz a second time.

Pour or shovel the mixture into your lined tray and put it in the oven to cook for 30 to 40 minutes. You'll know when it's cooked because the cake should just bounce back a little when you prod the top with your finger. Take it out of the oven and leave to cool on a wire rack to cool. When the cake is cold, remove it from the tin and cut into small squares. Portion it up into bags and freeze.

Best training treat ever

Tuna Cake

If liver is too rich for your dog you can make a tuna cake instead.

Drain a 250g can of tuna (tuna in oil works better in a food processor), blitz it in the blender or processor, then add the rest of the ingredients and repeat as for the liver cake. Makes equally smelly, so very good, training treats.

Birthday Cake

Well, I couldn't leave this section without adding a cake mix for special occasions. Use this recipe for special days. Makes enough for four dogs.

For the cake
4 eggs
200g peanut butter (the kind with no salt or sugar added)
50ml sunflower oil
50ml honey
2 medium carrots, grated
200g oat flour
1 tsp baking powder

For the icing
3 tbsp Greek yoghurt
1 ½ tbsp peanut butter

Preheat the oven to 180°C, 350°F or Gas 4. In a large bowl, combine the eggs, peanut butter, oil and honey and mix well. Stir in the grated carrot, then add the flour and baking powder and fold it into the mixture.

Pour the cake batter into a greased and lined cake tin and bake for 40 minutes. Leave it to cool on a wire rack for a few minutes, before turning it out of the tin.

When it is completely cool, you can add the icing. Simply combine the Greek yoghurt and peanut butter, put the mixture into the fridge for 20 minutes to stiffen a little, then spread it onto the cake with a pallet knife.

Job done

⟜ SMOOTHIES ⟞

Another good stand-by if you have a picky dog or a skinny one you're trying to fatten up. They're also very good frozen as treats to help your dog cool down on a hot day.

There's no hard and fast rule here – just keep the ingredients simple and few. Use whatever fruit or veg you have to hand as long as it's on the safe-for-dogs list. Use goats' milk rather than cow's milk, or water, for liquid.

Stick it all in a blender and whizz!

Banana Fruit Smoothie

½ banana
A handful of blueberries
100ml Toplife goats' milk
for dogs

Peanut Butter Smoothie

For a luxury treat and only a
little, as this one is pretty high
in calories

½ banana
1 tsp flaxseed
1 tsp peanut butter (the
kind with no added salt or
sugar)
Toplife goats' milk for
dogs to blend

Apple and Carrot Smoothie

1 apple, skin on, seeds
removed
1 carrot
Water to blend

Vitamin B Special

Dogs seem to like dark green
veggies, so while this one might
be a little bitter to you or me,
most dogs love it

A handful of kale
1 pear, skin on, seeds
removed
1 tsp coconut oil
Water to blend

see also simple wholesome treats on p88

Zero-effort
treat for
a hot day

 Raw food

If there's a more emotive subject in dog world than raw feeding I've yet to find it. Advocates of raw feeding can be evangelistic to the point of militancy. And the detractors (who, incidentally, tend to be at the professional end of the dog spectrum – vets and pet food companies) can be equally adamant. So no wonder some of you are unwilling to try giving your dog raw food: you're afraid you'll do your dog harm, or cop it from all sides for getting it wrong.

And then there's that group we don't see, armed with bags of common sense and going about their daily business, feeding their dogs raw food quite happily thank you. We can learn so much from this knowledgeable and dedicated group of dog owners.

Reasons to feed raw

Dog owners give many reasons as to why they feed raw but the most common are:

I like to know what I'm feeding my dog

She was ill for a long time but is no longer sick

She is so much healthier for it

His teeth gleam

His breath doesn't smell

His skin and coat glisten!

She doesn't have that doggie smell coming off her

Her poo is tiny because she's digesting what she eats

She doesn't itch and scratch like she used to

I hardly ever have to visit the vet any more because she just doesn't get sick

My dog doesn't have a pick of fat on him

It's a lot cheaper than feeding him a bag of dog food (once you know what you're doing)

It's what dogs and cats have evolved to eat (debatable)

Dogs are basically wolves (so the dog has evolved from wolves but their gut hasn't?)

You can tell from my last two points that I take some of this with a pinch of salt, but on the whole, if it agrees with him, I think raw is a fantastic way to feed your dog.

Two types of raw

The raw revolution started as a DIY movement, but inevitably the food manufacturers have moved in. The pros and cons of commercially produced and home-prepared raw foods are similar to those of commercial and home-produced cooked foods. If you buy frozen raw food from a pet food manufacturer, you can be sure of giving your dog a balanced diet. If you buy the ingredients of your dog's diet yourself, you will know what they are eating, but you'll have to give some thought to ensuring that the mix is balanced.

Commercially produced raw food

So there's a niche, which has been neatly filled by prepared, frozen raw foods from the likes of Nature's Menu, Natural Instinct, Honey's Real Dog Food and others. All have a wealth of knowledge behind them and will be happy to walk you through starting out on raw. Buy online or straight out of the freezer at good pet shops.

These prepared meals are a great compromise, nutritionally speaking. They are still uncooked but have been formulated to meet the requirements to be a complete food. So you know you're getting the right mix of protein, bone and veg and you can see clearly what's in the bag from the label. The only downside is that you need a freezer. The main hurdles for these brands, which will iron themselves out over the next few years, are that legislation and the major commercial pet food brands are challenging their safety from a human perspective – the salmonella risk in particular. So the road ahead will be a rocky one for commercial raw food but expect it to flourish all the same. And don't just settle for the cheapest thing you find online, or in a pet shop. When I was researching raw as an

option I came across the problem of ground bone in prepared foods. A few lovely customers on my Facebook page shared their own raw feeding experiences, explaining how finding a food with ground bone that was ground up finely enough proved to be a bit of an issue. In the end they went to raw feeding forums on the internet for advice, which duly came, and now they're sorted and happy with their raw food of choice, which pitches up on their doorstep every month, finely ground bone and all.

DIY raw

The hardcore raw fooders don't touch the commercial stuff. Their aim is to give their dog a diet as close as possible to the raw variety of a wild scavenger. Simply put, it comes down to feeding your dog raw food made up of some or all of the following: meat and fish, offal, bone, veg and fruit. It's not that hard to do, and undoubtedly, anatomically and physiologically, dogs and cats are more suited to raw food than cooked or processed foods, but it's definitely a lifestyle choice and if you want to do it yourself it takes time, commitment, effort on your part, research, tweaking to suit your dog, and a good bit of freezer space. How long it will take to convert your dog entirely over to raw will depend on his age, temperament and how long your dog has been fed a conventional diet. You should also check that there's no underlying condition or reason why your dog shouldn't be fed raw.

Changing over to raw - the basics

The key to changing your dog to raw food (or to any new diet for that matter) is patience and a positive attitude. The older the dog, the more entrenched she is with her current diet, the longer it may take to make the change. There are a few tips and tricks you can employ to ease the transition, not dissimilar to the tactics I listed earlier in this section. Depending on what model you're going for, the general rule of thumb is that a dog needs 2-3% of her bodyweight in food per day, so a 10kg dog will want between 200g and 300g of raw food daily. You'll work out what is the right amount for your dog as you go along. It will be roughly 70-80% meat muscle, 10-20% bone, 10% offal and 10% fruit and veg. And I mean roughly.

Making the switch. You can switch overnight from kibble to raw feeding if you like. If you want to move your dog over gradually, feed him a mix of raw and kibble, but give them separately as he will digest them at different rates and you want him to get used to these new textures. Gradually lessen the amount of kibble while increasing the raw food.

Act natural. Dogs can sense stress in their human at a hundred paces. So stay positive, act casual and try not to hover over them to see if they take to their new food.

Take your time. You don't have to rush this. You're making a change for the rest of their lives. It's a marathon, not a sprint. So chill. Leave your dog to get used to the new food. Doesn't matter if it takes all day.

One protein at a time. If you've been feeding your dog cooked chicken, move him on to fresh chicken. If it's been lamb, move over to that. This way you're not hitting him with flavours that he's unaccustomed to and you can introduce new proteins slowly over time. Equally, it's a good way of spotting food intolerances.

Start with meat only, no bone. You can introduce bone after a week or so.

Introduce offal slowly, in tiny amounts at first, after they've been on raw for a couple of weeks. Most dogs tolerate heart, kidney and liver, etc, very well, but on the off chance that they won't, start slow and small. As with everything, feed according to your dog's tolerance.

That's pretty much it. After that you can mix it up all you like. The key is to get the nutritional balance right and make sure they're not missing out, because they're not going to be getting food from anyone else to make up the difference. There are bags of feeding plans, recipes and information out there. You'll be fine!

Reading and research

There's a big debate going on if you want to find out more.

MANAGING CHANGE

When I speak to customers about their dogs' itching skin I always ask, 'What do you feed your dog?' Often, a change from a poor-quality food to a much better diet will improve their dogs' overall health no end. The answer that comes back invariably ends with the sentence: 'I tried to change his diet but the new food upset his tummy.' Of course it did. If you have been eating the same thing, day in, day out for years, anything new is bound to give you a little grief. But don't let that put you off; it's temporary – in most cases your dog will have adjusted within a couple of weeks, if not sooner. Isn't it worth it for a healthier, happier dog? (Do you see what I did there, with the guilt?)

Dog treats and chews

When I started My Itchy Dog, diet was a big factor for me in getting to the heart of why a dog was itching and scratching. I decided not to sell dog food, purely for commercial reasons – there's very little profit in it, what would I sell, how many varieties, in what sizes? Someone will always sell it for less than I can buy it for anyway and it costs a fortune to courier to customers. I'd have been out of business in weeks.

However, I was selling treats and I was determined that the selection of dog treats I stocked should be the best you could get – online or in a bricks and mortar pet shop – because research, experience and countless conversations had taught me that if a dog's being fed the best food out there, chances are the treats he's getting will be nothing short of garbage! I don't know why we do it – maybe it's because we equate the treats we give our dogs with the treats we give ourselves.

What I mean is, I know that bag of Maltesers is full of sugar and fat, and I should probably only eat one or two (who does that?) instead of eating the whole bag but I trough the lot regardless. So when we give the dog a treat we're even less likely to read the label and more likely to go by the colours and pretty pictures on the front of the packet. Or, worse, we use a treat to (supposedly) clean their teeth, help their creaky old joints or improve their coat condition, taken happily in by the promise that it will 'promote dental health' or, even more meaninglessly 'support your dog's mobility the delicious way!' What do those words even mean?

Good treats, bad treats

The good news about healthy dog treats is they don't have to cost any more than the unhealthy versions. This is because they're usually made by smaller companies, who don't blow the budget on marketing, but rather concentrate on the ingredients. Again, forget the hype on the front and read the label.

Shop for treats whose labels are listed by ingredients, not categories, and you'll be fine. You can get a great bag of papaya dog treats (ingredients – dried papaya – I know, it's a shocker) for £3.69 or a bag of 'dental' treats (ingredients – meat and animal derivatives, cereals, permitted colourants, etc.) for over £4.50 a bag. So very healthy treats don't cost a bomb. I'd stay away from rawhide that's been treated (although most of it has, so it needs to be washed at least) such as smoked rawhide or hide shoes with hide 'laces'. These are pretty efficient choke hazards in my view. Try a deer antler – they won't make a mess and they last for ages – or a juicy bone from the butcher if you're not worried about the floor.

Don't forget you can always give your dog a simple, fresh treat, like a piece of carrot, broccoli or a slice of pear. These are cheap and healthy options and you're likely to have some lying around (look underneath that bag of Maltesers).

Let me say it again: human treats are not to be used as dog treats, people! By that I mean Rich Tea biscuits, toast and jam, Yorkshire pudding with gravy, and leftover pizza, all of which at one time or another customers have told me the dog gets. Every night before bed, in the case of the toast!

Zero-effort dog treats

Fresh, raw bones

If your dog likes a bone (and most dogs do) find a butcher who'll either save one or get one in for you. I buy mine by the tray, for a couple of quid, and freeze them. Nikita loves them straight out of the freezer, especially on a warm day. Bones MUST be raw, as cooked bones splinter and are very dangerous for dogs. Go for bones that are larger than your dog's mouth, preferably full of marrow. She's then occupied for ages, scraping the marrow out, picking off bits of meat left on the bone, and allowing you to get on with your own stuff. If your dog is eating a bone in the garden, I'd either bring it in at night or discard it after she's done with it. That way you're not attracting foxes into the garden or parasites and flies onto the bone for your dog to revisit later.

A free-range egg, shell and all

No dog treat is easier to get your mitts on at short notice, or better for the dog. An egg, in its shell (maybe crack it just a little so your dog knows there's something worth working towards inside) once or twice a month, preferably outside(!) will do wonders for his skin and coat, brain and heart. An egg is a complete food, full of amino acids, vitamins A, B2, B6 and B12, iron, calcium, potassium and on and on. It is also one of the few foods in the world that naturally contains vitamin D.

Don't worry about salmonella – eggs are safe to eat, and a dog's saliva laughs in the face of such bacteria.

Variety is the spice of life and all that...

So there we are: three different ways to feed your dog, all of them with their own pros and cons. Ultimately, of course, it's down to what works best for you. But, whichever way you decide to go, try and maintain some variety in your dog's diet.

Yup, sorry, can open, worms everywhere... but I'm going to be bold and say this just one more time. In my view, feeding a dog the same food every day, apparently in the name of consistency, is a recipe for *all-out boredom*. Dogs love their food and relish the odd surprise and change – just like we do. And once you get started, believe me, you'll find that making a bit of an effort to keep the dog's meals interesting is both pleasurable and fun.

We feed ours a mixture of cooked

OTHER EASY HOME-MADE TREATS:

Meat and fish, simply cooked or raw, no added salt and no gravy either

Cooked sweet potato

Cooked peas

Berries of all types, fresh or frozen – contain good antioxidants

HOT-WEATHER TREATS

A slice of cold watermelon

Frozen fruit and veg

A frozen raw bone

Home-made chicken stock, frozen into ice cubes

food and very good wet food, with proper healthy treats and the odd bone. Nikita gets a bit of shop-bought raw and raw chicken drumsticks too. The only rule for me is that I don't mix raw and cooked food in the same meal.

Our much-loved and remembered lurcher, Bud, loved nothing more than a raw egg once in a while. He'd play with it, tease it along the patio floor, until he could bear it no longer, then crush it, eating contents and shell, leaving nothing behind. I also have some lovely photos of him lying down next to a lump of cucumber. He liked to gaze at it for a while before demolishing that too.

How to keep your dog in good health

·············· 🐾 ··············

(... as naturally as possible)

The word 'natural' is a hackneyed term overused to the point of being meaningless. Which is a shame, because there are some products out there that are all natural and do a great job of repelling fleas or clearing up wounds... We've just forgotten about them or didn't know they were there in the first place. Take apple cider vinegar, for instance. It's renowned for helping arthritis, relieving allergies, healing skin and clearing up infections. Bathe your dog's itchy paws in it once a day (use a 4-1 warm water to vinegar ratio) for a few days and that should put paid to the itch. Plus your dog will love the attention.

You may be reading this because you have exhausted all the options the vet has offered and you still have a sick dog, or you may want to explore the natural approach before seeking a vet's opinion.

It's not an either/or situation

Just so we're clear, I am not anti-vet; but I prefer a more rounded approach. I have great respect for what they do for a living. I couldn't do it. I took my cat Pearl to the vet once with a suspected abscess. She was scared and jumped off the table at the first opportunity. The abscess burst on landing! Blood and pus everywhere. You could tell she felt better instantly. I nearly hurled. The vet just laughed, cleaned out the abscess and sent me on my way. Yes, there are times when only a trip to the vet will do. Ultimately, though, I prefer the holistic, all-round approach when it comes to my pets' wellbeing. And the feedback I get from customers using natural where appropriate – and it's appropriate a lot of the time – is that you can get really good results, cut down on vet visits and, thereby, on the expense and stress.

In the end it's all about personal choice. I chose to vaccinate my pets early on but not vaccinate after that, preferring a titre test (see p145). They haven't had pharmaceutical flea treatment and monthly wormers... for years! And they don't have fleas or worms. But BB did recently get a course of antibiotics for a kidney infection, his first in a long while, because that was what was required.

From my experience of talking to my customers, I suspect it's partly your inquisitive nature and partly exasperation that's led you here.

Brace yourselves. This is a longish chapter, designed to be a dip-in-and-out affair, depending on what ails your dog at the time. First, I'm going to work through the top 10 reasons your dog will visit the vet in his or her lifetime and how you can treat each one of these problems naturally – meander through this section and find what you need, as and when. Then I move on to a few other common conditions, and the life stages of pregnancy and old age, as well as the important matter of saying goodbye. After that, it's allergies – why we are plagued by them, and how to manage them – and finally the slightly vexed question of food supplements – whether dogs need them, and how to spot one that works.

The TOP 10 reasons your dog will visit the vet — and how you can treat each problem naturally

Listed below are the top 10 canine health issues, compiled recently by market researchers using data gathered from pet insurance claims, veterinary practice records and dog owners themselves. In fact, these have always been the most common reasons why dogs end up being hefted on to the treatment room table.

What I hope to offer here is an alternative way of treating your dog. Because, believe me, by taking a step back and looking at your dog as a whole (feeding him well, looking after his mental health and physical welfare, bolstering his natural defences against parasites and adding supplements to his food), you should find that many of these common health problems are entirely preventable, while the others are easily managed by using simple, natural methods at home.

I'll trot out the old proverb of 'an ounce of prevention is worth a pound of cure' again because it's so completely and utterly true. Less is more, and all that. As always, though, if you're worried about something, and it's not a problem that you can tackle, see a vet.

🐾 An ear infection 🐾

Dogs with long ears, narrow ear canals or allergy sufferers are more prone to ear problems but most will have an issue at some point or another. Bacteria and excess yeast are primary causes of ear infections in dogs. Chuck in your ear mites, cysts, tumours, trapped water, grass seeds, a build-up of ear wax and too much ear hair and it's no wonder dogs' ears are number one on the list.

Given that he is likely to have to submit to having his ears poked around with at some point, it's a good idea to get your dog used to having his ears touched when there isn't a problem so that he's not inclined to bite you when there is and you need to have a look inside. If you like cleaning a dog's ears, and your dog likes having them cleaned, the satisfaction to effort ratio is out of this world. Especially if your dog is a dirt magnet. The best tip I had from my vet was 'only clean where you can actually see – don't ever push anything down into the ear canal.' So I don't. Good advice. And she had a 'don't mess with me' look in her eye, which I respect enormously.

Lily the
Wonder
Dog

Signs your dog has an ear problem

More ear scratching than usual
Smelly ears
Head shaking
Redness or wounds inside the ear flap
Rubbing ears along the floor or walls
Hair loss around the ear
Hearing loss
Any discharge

Ways to prevent an ear infection

Check ears regularly for smells, mites, dirt or wax build-up
Clean them if they appear dirty
Dry ears thoroughly but gently after a bath or swimming
Remove excess ear hair or ask the groomer to do it for you

The main causes of ear problems

Acute Infections

A bacterial infection, due to a bite, cut or scratch that has become infected, either inside or outside the ear.

Treatment:
Neem oil

Rub a small amount of organic neem oil on to the wound a couple of times a day until healed. If you suspect a wound, but can't see it because it's too far down into the ear, it's off to the vet.

Chronic Infections

This is more a long-term thing, common among allergy sufferers and dogs who have a weakened immune system, caused by stress or overuse of antibiotics (eg *Candida*).

Treatment:
Neem oil
Apple cider vinegar
Echinacea

Neem oil and apple cider vinegar both have good antibiotic properties. Use the neem oil on reddened, sore areas and open wounds. Use the vinegar diluted with warm water as a soothing wash inside ears and ear flaps. This is lovely mixed with cool water (not freezing cold) for relief on a hot day too.

If your dog has a weakened immune system caused by stress, a period of illness or long-term use of medication, then a short course of an echinacea supplement will help strengthen the body and enable it to fend off infections.

Ear mites

Ear mites present in the ears as a reddish-brown waxy substance which can easily be mistaken for dirt. Wipe a bit out with your finger if you can stomach it (I love it, but I'm weird) and rub it between your fingers. If it's greasy it's probably ear mites.

Treatment:
Colloidal silver drops
Thornit canker powder

Either clean the ears out with colloidal silver and an ear-cleaning cloth or dust the inside of the inner ear with Thornit powder. Both have good antibacterial properties. My personal choice is silver drops because I can drop them down into the ear and let them work away in places I can't (and wouldn't want to) poke about in, and it's less messy. Either will work just fine, though.

Dave the cat used to get ear mites, no idea why; he never attracted fleas, ticks or other parasites but ear mites made a beeline for him. Luckily for me, he loved having his ears cleaned – I think it just made them feel so much better afterwards. There's nothing like sticking a wodge of kitchen towel doused in colloidal silver into your cat's ear and for him to ram his head as hard as he can into your finger for maximum satisfaction. Like I said, I'm weird.

Fungus!

If you smell a yeasty odour when you put your nose to your dog's ear then it's probably a fungal problem like *Candida*. When *Candida* in the gut proliferates unchecked it can lead to a yeast overgrowth, which often turns up in the ears.

Treatment:
YumPro probiotics
Colloidal silver drops
Neem oil
A change of diet

Add a probiotic, short-term, to your dog's diet and eliminate sugars and over-processed carbohydrates for a while. It's back to reading those labels for you. Clean the ears daily for a few days with colloidal silver drops and an ear cloth or apply a thin film of neem oil to any red or spotty patches.

Blockages

These can be caused by excess hair and wax build-up, grass seeds or water.

Just like old men, dogs, especially those which don't moult – Bedlington terriers, poodles, bichon frises, for example – collect ear hair like some people collect stamps. Not only that but when it gets tangled up with excess earwax you're on your way to a great ear-cleaning session!

Treatment:
Regular cleaning
Clipping ear hair
A trip to the groomer

If you think there is a foreign body, such as a grass seed, in your dog's ear, then, unless it's so loose and near the top of the ear you can't fail, take him to the vet or groomer to get it removed.

HOW TO CLEAN THE EARS

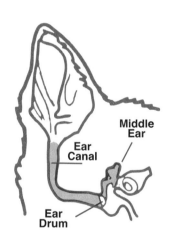

Middle Ear

Ear Canal

Ear Drum

When you look down into the ear canal you'll see it just appears to stop at a dead end. In actual fact, the ear canal is just turning at a right angle towards your dog's head. Don't ever clean any part you can't see. Never try to go around the bend with any foreign object.

You can do a simple wash with salt water or apple cider vinegar diluted with warm water. Or, for itchy, mucky ears, colloidal silver eardrops work very well. Squeeze a few drops from a dropper bottle into your dog's ear and quickly start to massage the base of the ear from the outside. Keep a firm hold on the dog while you do this otherwise you'll end up picking bits of ear crud off your nice clean shirt as the dog shakes her head. Next, clean out the ear (only as far as you can see, no poking about) with an ear cloth, a ball of cotton wool or soft kitchen paper. Get as much crud out as you can.

Then let the dog go and stand well back. Shaking her head vigorously will bring more waxy dirt up from the depths, which you can then clear out with more cotton wool. I find it revolting but oddly satisfying. This whole matter is probably best dealt with outside, come to think of it.

If your dog is of the hair-growing, non-moulting variety, you're probably a regular at the groomers, anyway, so ask them to pay special attention to ear cleaning, and clean their ears on a regular basis at home. You can add a little light clipping of ear hair to your routine to maintain airflow inside the ear. Ask your groomer to show you a safe way to do it.

🐾 A skin problem 🐾

So here we are. We've landed at my personal favourite thing, the whole reason I started www.myitchydog.co.uk.

Now the skin is the largest organ a dog has, and it's a marvellous, sophisticated piece of kit. It grows hair, feeds parasites and has a nice covering of *Candida albicans* (yeast) that peacefully cohabits until something sets it off. However, unlike we humans who can sweat all over, as anyone stuck on the Tube or train on a hot day can attest, dogs only sweat from the pads of their paws and the nose. They pant to release heat and cool down, but that's not sweating. So their skin, unencumbered by sweat, holds onto stuff – dirt, dander and the like – making it a feeding and breeding ground for all sorts of parasites. Dog skin is the gift that keeps on giving, to a critter.

The time of year really matters when it comes to itching. When I tell you that I sell far fewer products for itchy skin in winter but sales take off like a rocket the minute the sun comes out and the trees begin to blossom, most of you will nod your heads sagely as you mash yet another antihistamine into your dogs' food.

Itching and scratching somewhat is normal; it's when scratching or paw chewing becomes constant and obsessive that you know something's not right, and dogs will scratch for a number of reasons. There is plenty you can do to minimise itching and scratching so take heart, all is far from lost.

The main reasons your dog itches and scratches

1. **Fleas, ticks and mites** – tiny little parasitic critters, super-itchy, sometimes seasonal, always dementing.

2. **Atopic canine dermatitis** – or atopy. An inhaled allergy – pollens from trees, flowers, grasses and plants, or mould spores – set it off.

3. Fungus – an overgrowth of *Candida albicans* on the skin, or malassezia, a very itchy fungal infection.

4. Household chemicals – cleaning and laundry products.

5. Grooming products – especially the cheaper shampoos.

6. Air fresheners – research shows that babies and dogs can suffer depression, upset tummies and skin allergies to air fresheners, because they're much closer to the ground than we are. The plug-in, automatic sprays are the worst offenders.

Fleas, ticks and mites

Fleas, ticks and mites are disgusting. They suck up to our pets – taking blood, spreading disease, laying eggs, making new parasites by the thousand and leaving them all over the house. Immature fleas give our dogs tapeworm, too. No, fleas, ticks and mites are not a happy part of the dog landscape.

Fleas

Most of the fleas you'll find pimping off your dog are actually cat fleas.

They have flatter heads, all the better for moving swiftly through a dog's fur. Fleas are opportunists, they'll jump on to any mammal if there's a free blood meal going. And if they can get a two-for-one deal by laying eggs on their host at the same time, then so much the better. All aboard!

You'll know your dog's got fleas when you find him chewing his paws and pads, and scratching at his groin, armpits, belly or under his chin where he lies down, either on the floor or in his bed.

And what you need to know is that for every flea you spot on your dog there are nine more elsewhere, in your house, at various stages of development, and that you will have to treat the whole house to make sure they're all dealt with. Prevention is way easier to deal with than infestation.

This is how it works. A female flea lays up to 50 eggs a day on your dog. Flea eggs are white and a bit smaller than a grain of rice. The eggs get shaken off as your dog goes about his business to land

on the carpet, his bed (or yours), and in between floorboards. In a few days or weeks, larvae hatch.

The larvae move along using tiny hairs on their bodies, finding food – dirt, flea faeces and dust – which as we know is mostly human skin: is yours crawling yet? When large enough, they spin themselves into a protective cocoon to develop into an adult, just like a moth or a butterfly, where they wait... and wait... and wait. Until it's 'time'. While the adult flea is safely tucked up inside its cocoon, it's golden. It can hunker down in there for months, years, until the conditions are right for it to hatch for maximum effect. The adult flea only emerges if it's pretty sure there's a host close by. It detects this by vibration, changes in temperature or even carbon dioxide levels as your pet breathes into the carpet.

As a for instance, I bought a flat in 1999, moved in and no hint of a flea. In 2001 I got my cats Pearl and Dave from the most excellent Celia Hammond Trust which was just down the road. Well. Within two weeks that flat was jumping. And yet the cats had been free and clear of worms and fleas before they came to me – I gave my cats fleas! Who does that? The pupae had been hiding in the carpet all this time; it's the only thing the previous owners left behind, that and a really skanky sofa I ditched on day one. One whiff of a furry coat was all it took to wake them up and invite them to jump aboard. Flea pupae are ticking parasite time bombs. Fact.

Ticks

This has got to be the most bottom-clenching parasite of the lot. The two most common ticks found in the UK are deer or sheep ticks (in the countryside) and hedgehog ticks (more urban) but a tick is a tick is a tick; it will hop onto anyone it can leech a meal off. In the garden you'll find ticks on foxes, squirrels and blackbirds as well as on the aforementioned hedgehogs.

Ticks are the consummate traveller. Compact, self-contained and discreet – they move from place to place, practically unseen. A tick will be sitting on a leaf, minding its own business, next to a well-worn path, when your dog comes snuffling about, as dogs are inclined to do. The tick, feeling a bit peckish, will hop onto your dog and make its way to a part of your dog's body that's nice and warm and not too furry. Now it settles down to eat. And this is the horror film part.

A tick has no head, contrary to popular belief; it doesn't need one. The tick makes a pit in the skin – the longer it stays there the deeper the pit. The pit is a reservoir for collecting the blood. Once settled in, it releases a cement-like substance that sets, making the tick harder to remove.

A tick can suck blood for up to two days in one sitting. It feeds by anaesthetising an area of skin and cutting into it. It then inserts a barbed feeding tube into the hole and starts to suck. As well as blood it's also sucking up any disease pathogens its host is carrying, to pass on to the next host, or injecting disease into its host as its saliva passes down the feeding tube. When it's satiated, the tick drops off and moves on to the next stage of development.

So ticks spread disease, and if they're not carrying any, the bite itself will get infected if left untreated. Risk of infection is greatest in spring and summer in the UK – the most common tick-borne infection being Lyme disease (borreliosis), which is spreading quite rapidly. The Health Protection Agency (HPA) now monitors Lyme disease and since 2010 it has become a requirement of every microbiology lab to report any diagnoses of it. Any mammal is susceptible, so use the information in this chapter to protect your dog, yourself and anyone you go a-wandering with.

Lyme disease bacteria migrate into the connective tissues in the body, spread out and eventually enter the heart, joints and brain tissue. The infection weakens your immune response, so the first thing you know about it is when your dog appears under the weather.

WHY TICKS ARE LIKE A PYRAMID SCHEME

Ticks are the soul of generosity when it comes to spreading disease. A tick will bite an animal, pass bacteria on to it while feeding, then hop off and leave town. That animal then becomes a reservoir of bacteria which it passes on to all the other ticks which make a stop at the 'suck my blood, why don't you!' cafe that is the fox, hedgehog, bird, etc.

All those ticks are now infected. They pass the disease on to anyone they bite – you, me, the dog or that hapless sheep over there. So one infected tick passes bacteria on to 10 other ticks. Those 10 ticks then infect 10 other animals a piece and so on. A pyramid scheme. And we all know how they end!

If you have the presence of mind, keep any tick you remove, bag it and freeze it, not forgetting to put the date on the bag. That way, if your dog gets sick even after a few weeks the vet can test it to rule out or diagnose a tick-borne disease quickly.

Neat, eh?

Mites

I've added a section on mites, even though you keep them down in precisely the same way as you would fleas and ticks, because the symptoms of the different types vary so much. Each species has its own target audience – ears, food bins, etc; they can arrive at different times of the year – for example, harvest mites in August; they look different and cause anything from a minor irritation to a horrendous infection. So I'm sorry if this section is a long one but there's just so much to know.

Mites thrive in warm, humid conditions. Our homes and gardens, our own bodies. Certain types of mite can live on our skin quite happily. They don't bother us and we don't bother them. Having said that, the mites that bug us the most are:

House dust mites
Surface mites
Storage mites
Ear mites
Harvest mites

House dust mites

House dust mites cause skin allergies, dermatitis, asthma and rhinitis in dogs, cats and humans. They account for most of the mite allergies in the UK. Symptoms in dogs are constant itching and scratching, fur loss, runny eyes and nose, and sneezing.

House dust mites are tiny, opaque creatures, unseen with

the naked eye. They like our homes very much, thank you, especially our bedrooms. Mites eat our detritus, mostly our dead, shed skin. So you will find them anywhere there is dust. If your house is anything like ordinary there will be a lot of dust. If you're not totally grossed out already, they love a bed, especially a pillow, because of the proximity to our sweaty bodies, which make the humidity levels just right. Think about that the next time you wake up drooling into your pillow.

Surface mites – 'walking dandruff'

A great name for an overstayer. The surface mite lives on a host for its entire life-cycle of 21 days. To give it its proper name, the Cheyletiella mite lives on the top layer, or surface, of your dog's skin. It's a highly contagious mite too. As it feeds it pushes flakes of surface skin around, hence the nickname 'walking dandruff'. Symptoms can range from dandruff, moving or not, and intense itching and scratching, to hair loss, especially along the back.

Storage mites

I get a lot of calls from dog owners saying their dogs have developed an allergy to storage mites. This is a pretty simple one to fix, and nowhere near as common as house dust mites. Storage mites can be present in anything that can go mouldy – grain, dry pet food, cereals, cheese – and they're a real pest for agriculture for that reason.

The allergic reaction is sometimes referred to in humans as Baker's Lung or Grocer's Itch!

If you have a dog who's itchy all the time, not seasonally as with harvest mites, for example, then storage mites will come a close second after house dust mites as a possible culprit. Look out for hair loss on the face, around the eyes, muzzle and under the chin. Also excessive sneezing, and possibly asthma.

Dry dog food doesn't come with storage mites included (at no extra cost to you, dear dog owner); the mites infest the dog food once you get it home and open the bag. The best way to keep on top of storage mites is to either feed wet food instead, or buy dry food in smaller amounts. When you get the bag home, store it in an airtight plastic container, and always clean this thoroughly in hot, soapy water before tipping in a new bag.

Ear mites

Ear mites are generally much more of a problem for cats but dogs get them too. You can usually tell your dog or cat is being bothered by them when they adopt the Yoda pose, as I like to call it, by flattening one or both ears at a 45 degree angle to the head.

However, ear mites are extremely contagious so if one dog's got it, chances are so will any other animals they cuddle up to, and they will all need treating. An ear mite infestation is pretty easy to sort out and keep on top of. See the section on how to treat ear infections, above, and the one on how to keep your dog's ears clean and ear mite-free.

Harvest mites – red dust

The harvest mite is a member of the tick family. It's another seasonal mite, especially pesky during the seasonal change from summer into autumn. Harvest mites can be found in woodland, long grass, parks and gardens. It's not the adult mite that does that biting, though; it's the larvae that do the damage. Kids, eh?

Harvest mites, in their larval stage, swarm and feed, causing intense itching. You will recognise harvest mite larvae as a red dust clinging to your dog's hair. The itching is caused by a digestive enzyme in the larvae's saliva. They feed for 2-3 days, increasing in size 3-4 times before dropping off.

Unlike other mites, harvest mites like sunny, dry spots and heat. To keep them at bay, try moving on to early-morning or evening walks, and avoid long grass.

Mange mites – sarcoptic and demodectic

You've probably used the term 'mangy' to describe a tatty-looking fox you've seen around and about, I always think well-loved teddy bears have a mangy look about them due to their patchy fur loss. If I suspected my dog had mange, I would definitely get it diagnosed by a vet because the likelihood is that it's already developed into a bacterial infection by the time I can see it.

There are two types of mange – Sarcoptes mites burrow into the skin, while Demodex mites live on hair follicles.

Both types of mange can occur when a dog has a compromised immune system, for example because of prolonged steroid use. Starving dogs and foxes are often overtaken by mange mites. Domestic dogs in the UK can catch mange after coming into contact with a fox who has it. A puppy, who hasn't yet developed a mature immune system, is also at risk of catching mange from its mother.

Sarcoptic mange is highly contagious and skin can quickly become infected. The mite burrows through the skin, opening it up to infection, and causing intense itching and crusting, especially on the elbows and in the ears. Depending on the extent of the infection, your dog may need antibiotics.

As mange mites often overtake an animal due to its low immunity, I would have to take a good look at why this has happened. I'd look at nutrition, and the stress levels in the environment.

Demodectic mange mites aren't anything like as contagious because they live at the base of hair, in the follicles, so they are buried deep in your dog's fur. As long as you have a healthy dog, these particular mites can live on your dog quite happily, just as the mites on our skin do (you really do have mites that live off your skin, trust me).

But when the dog's immune system is overburdened, through long-term illness for example, it can get out of control and demodectic mites will be found in huge numbers under a microscope. It's thought that it's actually bacteria that cause demodex mange – the mites prepare the ground, so to speak. Look out for hair loss around the eyes, muzzle and forelegs.

Treatment for fleas, ticks and mites

The treatment for all these little blighters is pretty much the same. I will give a general rundown on this first, and then offer more particular information on the removal of ticks, how to deal with flea bite allergies, and – absolutely crucial! – how to rid your house of pests and keep it pest-free.

Neem shampoo (Skinny Dip shampoo is great)
Neem oil (Ekoneem)

A good wash in neem is vital if your dog has fleas or mites. Wash your arms with neem shampoo before washing the dog so the fleas don't hop on you too. Lather up the dog and leave him in it for up to 10 minutes to kill live creatures and their eggs. You need to wash the whole dog, obviously, so make sure you use a shampoo that can be used on the face *.

After rinsing and drying your dog well, chuck the towel into a hot wash immediately. You can give the dog another wash a couple of days later if he's still itching. In the case of fleas, in particular, you should comb out afterwards for any dead bugs or eggs. For both flea and tick bites, I recommend rubbing in a bit of Ekoneem, which has antibiotic properties and will soothe the itching. Some dogs become hypersensitive to flea bites and then react every time they get bitten. The saliva in a flea bite irritates the skin, which can become intensely itchy. Again, a thin application of pure organic neem oil twice a day should clear it up in about 48 hours. It will take the itch away almost at once.

* I had a customer who called to tell me she'd managed to wash all of her dog but missed the bit under his chin. She found fleas taking refuge there a couple of days later and had to repeat the process again, adding the chin this time. Their own furry desert island, washed away on a tsunami of neem suds.

'But I like fox poo!'

Lazy
Sunday
afternoon

HOW TO REMOVE A TICK SAFELY

There are only two ways. Both cheap and simple. Use either a fine-tipped pair of tweezers or an O'Tom Tick Twister.

Eyebrow tweezers are no good because they're too blunt; you want to touch the tick as little as possible. A pair of precision tweezers can be bought from craft shops or online for about £8. Or pick up an O'Tom Tick Twister for about £6 from the vet or online. Tick Twisters come in a set of two, one smaller than the other. They can be washed and reused and are recyclable. I keep a set in the house and one in the glove box.

The way to remove a tick using tweezers is firm and straight. Grab the tick with the tweezers at its closest point to the skin of the host and pull it straight up. Make it a smooth but firm movement. Don't squeeze or twist.

The reason you can twist using the Tick Twister is because it supports the tick; it doesn't grab it as tweezers do, so there's no pressure on the tick's mouth parts. Twisting in one direction only will free the proboscis from the skin. Twisting also loosens the cement-like saliva the tick uses to stick itself to the host before it starts to feed. You should never use the Tick Twister to lever the tick out, though; that will leave mouthparts behind. Whichever method you use, after removal wash the affected area with soap and water, then apply a little neem oil to the bite and wash your hands thoroughly.

WHAT NOT TO DO

Don't try and smother a tick with Vaseline, nail polish, soap or anything else for that matter. While it's trying to wriggle out it can send blood back into the host

Don't try to burn off a tick – it will drop off leaving mouthparts behind, which can get infected. And you'll set the dog alight!

You can't freeze a tick bite off. Again, panic will just cause it to disgorge its contents back into the dog.

A tick doesn't have a screw top. Don't try to twist out a tick unless you're using an O'Tom Tick Twister; you want to pull a tick out clean and straight.

If the mouthparts break off you won't be able to retrieve them because you can't see them with the naked eye.

You shouldn't ever try to pull out a tick with your fingers.

Neither should you do it with a pair of ordinary tweezers.

How to rid your house of pests

If you've got a flea on the dog, there will likely as not be more in the house. So you need to deal with that too. First things first: gather up all the dog bedding, any blankets she frequents, any toys that can be washed with them, and stick them in the washing machine. Wash everything on the highest temperature the label says you can and put them on a full wash, none of your eco-setting malarkey – we want those critters drowned, not just coming out needing a gentle tumble-dry and a bit of counselling.

The next thing is to spray the house. If you have fleas in the house (and you will have mites too) you need to clean up quickly so they don't hop straight back

on the dog. To get rid of fleas quickly, and I speak from experience, use what works. I would go for something like an Indorex spray as my first port of call; get it from your vet. It will kill adult fleas, stop their larvae and eggs in their tracks, and as an added bonus kill off any dust mites too. Spray as per the directions and that will get you a long way to a clean house.

When that's had time to do its stuff, you can move on to a good hoover and steam. If you have pets then you're probably already in possession of a decent hoover. Now is its finest hour. Break out the bag of attachments and go mad on the furniture – the sofa, bed frames, bookcases, skirting boards, rugs, curtains and blinds, in between the spindles on the bannisters, in the cracks between floorboards, and all hard flooring. Leave no stone unturned.

As gadgets go, you can't beat a floor steamer for killing bugs. Use it on hard floors, and carpets too, believe it or not. A shot of boiling steam is an ideal way of killing any remaining mites because you are relying on heat, not chemicals, to kill them, so you won't be leaving nasty residues on the floor to further agitate your dog's paws.

Finally, put some of your neem shampoo in warm water and wipe down all your hard edges that haven't been sprayed – cupboards, etc. The neem residue will keep on working.

After you've done all that, get someone else to cook dinner while you go and have a long, hot soak in the bath.

How to keep your house pest-free – naturally

Having banished an infestation with some of the strong stuff, as I suggest above, you should be able to keep on top of pest control without further recourse to pharmaceuticals. All that's required is a bit of regular attention and care.

DIY neem spray
Use this to spray your dog, house, decking and plants in spring. You can buy it ready-made (Skinny Spray); or make up your own, as per this little recipe.

Take 5ml of cold-pressed neem oil (I recommend Ekoneem), put it in a plant spray bottle and add 250ml of lukewarm water. Add a drop or two of washing-up liquid to bind the two together. Shake vigorously (the bottle, not you, obviously). Now spray a fine mist on everything – both inside and out. Make sure to use it up within 24 hours as the water will start to degrade the neem after that.

Make an easy flea trap
When I posted this on my blog, I got more likes and shares than on almost anything else before or since. It works!

Get yourself a shallow dish, a clean cat-food dish or a plant-pot tray is ideal. Fill it halfway with water and a little washing-up liquid and swish it about with your fingers to disperse the soap. Put it down on the floor, where it can't be kicked or tipped up, near to a plug socket, but not so close that water will get into the socket if it does get kicked over. Plug a night light into the socket and go to bed. Fleas will be attracted to the light, jump into the dish and get wet. Soapy water is kryptonite to a flea, which is now rendered powerless and drowns.

In the morning come downstairs (you'll feel like it's Christmas morning and you're five again) to count your dead fleas. Throw this water away and repeat nightly until you wake up one morning and discover there are no dead fleas floating about. I promise you, all this hard work will pay off in spades.

IN PRAISE OF NEEM

If you buy one product for your dog healthcare shelf, make it this wonder oil. Good Lord, it's brilliant stuff. Not only that but neem is one of only a handful of plants that has been very well researched, and papers published and peer-reviewed for its efficacy. India even won a patent/biopiracy war over it.

I like Ekoneem oil because it's pure, organic, and smells like cabbage on the turn. Which is what you want. If you get neem that smells lovely, and it's not mixed with anything else much that could account for the lovely smell, I'd be suspicious about its usefulness: it's its active ingredients that make it stink so if they have been synthesised out to make it more attractive to the consumer, it's not likely to be any good.

Neem oil is produced from the seeds of the neem tree, *Azadirachta Indica*, a member of the mahogany family. The best stuff comes from India and should be cold-pressed for maximum effect. Neem oil is antibacterial, anti-fungal and a powerful parasite repellent. It's even used as a contraceptive in India and Madagascar by both men and women. And, no, it's not the smell that puts lovers off. Studies show that neem, eaten in capsule form, kills sperm but doesn't affect fertility. Its effects are reversed after a few weeks when you stop taking them.

We use neem oil on the inside of BB's ear flaps when they get very itchy. She sometimes scratches them until they bleed when we're not looking. If she's been on her own for a couple of hours she can do some damage, so we rub a thin layer of Ekoneem pure neem oil onto the red, sore bits and hey presto, instant relief.

Nikita's neuter incision wasn't healing very well; it had actually started to come apart at one end. Two applications of Ekoneem a day for three days and it was gone. I'm not kidding when I say this stuff is amazing.

Neem oil is something that everyone should keep a pot of in the fridge. Use it on dogs and cats; a thin application is all you need. Because it's a vegetable oil and not an essential oil it's not going to do much harm if it's licked off. It's good for treating bites, burns, wounds, scratches, sore bits, dry spots, hot spots and sweet itch in horses too. I use it myself on mosquito bites, eczema and cuts, and it's great for nits, as my godchildren can attest...

'I see no ships!'

Other tips for keeping your house free of parasites:

Check your dog regularly for fleas or mites, and treat if necessary

Keep floors free of dirt and dust

Hoover the furniture and upholstery once in a while

Wash the dog's bedding and washable toys regularly

Bring toys in from the garden overnight to keep them away from flea-ridden foxes

Move your dog on to a good herbal flea, tick and mite preventative treatment

As I say, we do have to keep on top of the parasites. And if your dog has become overrun with them, there's no doubt that a strong pharmaceutical treatment is the way to go. Having dealt with the immediate problem, though – and despite what the four caring corporate giants that own more than 70% of the parasite treatment business around the world will tell you – it is entirely possible to control fleas by using a simple herbal food supplement.

The best product I have found by a country mile is the aptly named Billy No Mates from CSJ. It's so good I now buy it by the pallet-load in advance of the flea season kicking off, around early spring, so I don't run out. I should point out that I have no shares in this company; I just

think they make really good products, and this one is made in the UK, too.

Billy No Mates is basically a herbal blend of neem, lemon balm, mint, seaweed and fenugreek. If you hold the pot up to your nose you get a warm, sweet smell.

What makes it so effective? I hear you ask. Firstly, the neem – this is the key parasite repellent. Neem doesn't actually kill fleas, but it does repel them. It also acts on the flea's hormones, inhibiting its growth and its egg-laying capabilities. Fleas will drop off an animal that is eating neem, if they latch on at all.

Secondly, the other ingredients promote good gut health. The healthier the dog, the better at repelling he is. I know: I nag. Seaweed contains iodine, good for the thyroid in small doses, and has been linked to helping deter worms from taking up residence. Fenugreek is a natural anti-inflammatory, while lemon balm is used in herbal medicine for the cleansing of the gastrointestinal tract,

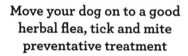

the liver and bile duct. It's also used for disorders of the central nervous system. So you're repelling fleas and other pests and helping your dog to get his internal house in order, gut-wise. Your dog will develop a very sleek and shiny coat into the bargain.

To prevent parasites becoming resistant to herbs it's a good idea to stop feeding them when the weather gets cold, at least for a few weeks. There are far fewer fleas about the place in winter so it shouldn't be a problem. You can always spray a little neem onto bedding in the interim.

Atopic canine dermatitis

This tends to be a seasonal problem, at its worst in spring and summer when the pollen is doing its thing. Your dog will be constantly scratching all over, possibly with runny eyes and nose, with wheezing and coughing added on for good measure.

Treatment:
Omega oils
Neem shampoo
Damp rub

A good oil blend added to your dog's food will help mitigate the effects on the skin of hay fever and other breathed-in allergies – Yumega Plus is a great one (see p177). Wash him with a neem shampoo or any shampoo based on essential oils which have antihistamine properties – sage, lemongrass, rosemary oils, for example, will reduce itching straight away. Avoid shampoos containing sodium lauryl or sodium laureth sulphates; they're too harsh and will strip the helpful oils from the skin and fur. Also, a good rub-down after coming in from a walk, either with a cool, damp flannel or a wet wipe with a good pH, but no parabens or petroleum derivatives, will remove much of the dander and pollens that set him off.

Fungus

We have a fine layer of *Candida albicans* in our gut and all over our bodies, and so do dogs. If your dog's immune system and gut have been weakened by illness or a poor diet, an overgrowth of *Candida* can flare up on the skin's surface causing red and very itchy spots and patches – mostly in humid places – inside ears, in between the toes, in skin creases, armpits and groin areas.

Treatment:
Less carbohydrate
Probiotics
Neem shampoo
Neem and coconut cream

Fungus gets the two-pronged attack. First, cut out the cheap, overprocessed carbs and sugars in their food. Stick to a good diet, grain-free if you can, with more protein from fish and meat, and less cereal and rice. Add a short-term probiotic to their food for a couple of weeks – Yumpro is good.

Then, tackle the external flare-up by washing your dog in a good neem shampoo and applying a soothing neem and coconut cream – Skinny Cream is brilliant. This is what I used to treat Nikita

when she arrived. She was riddled with malassezia and was just getting over her mange. It cleared her skin up a treat and wasn't harsh, so didn't sting.

The one thing I will say about clearing up fungal problems with neem is that fungus likes a fight. It may well flare up once you apply the neem and can get fairly lairy for a couple of days. But the neem always wins, so don't panic or give up. Keep on with it and you'll win the battle and the war.

Household chemicals

If you've got a dog who's really sensitive to cleaning products there is plenty you can do to help. Some of it sounds a bit drastic but you can make the changes over time, as and when things get replaced.

Treatment:
Ekoneem shampoo bar
A set of Pawz boots
Floor steamer
Carpet washer

This is normally a skin problem that affects the parts of a dog that touch the floor, a contact allergy: paw pads, bellies, groins and armpits, mostly. If you have pets you will probably already have a great vacuum cleaner to deal with the onslaught of pet hair. Vax, Miele and Dyson work really well. Don't use any carpet fresheners; just hoover. If you can wash the carpets once in a while, preferably with a shampoo for allergy sufferers, then do. I picked up a second-hand Vax carpet cleaner on eBay recently, so it doesn't have to cost a bomb.

If you have wooden or laminate

flooring, a floor steamer is going to be your new best friend. It's like a steam iron and a mop combined. The beauty of it is it doesn't need any cleaning products added and steam renders all allergens useless. It can also be used on carpets.

As for your poor dog's sore bits, there is a shampoo bar made by Ekoneem. – the Ekoneem shampoo bar, funnily enough – that's so gentle and has so few ingredients it won't sting your dog's sore paws. Because it's a bar you can just target the areas in need by rubbing it directly on to pre-wetted skin and fur. It's genius for reducing inflammation and taking the itch right out.

If the allergy becomes a really bad problem, Pawz make little socks from rubber so fine they resemble balloons before you blow them up – get them from www.collarways.com . They come in various sizes and offer protection from chemicals and slippery floors as they're super-grippy. In fact, even when their dogs don't have allergy problems, I've heard owners raving about these, saying their dogs are now happy to walk on floors they were previously scared to venture onto as they no longer slip and slide about.

Grooming products

Whether you're buying shampoos and spritzes to groom a dog yourself, or you happily hand Rover over to the groomer on a Saturday morning to be washed, dried, clipped and snipped while you treat yourself to the papers and breakfast out, it matters not. A good groomer will use whichever product you specify, and any dog with sensitive skin needs a gentle shampoo that won't aggravate them.

There are some excellent skin products out there for sensitive dogs these days. And you definitely get what you pay for. Look for products free from sodium lauryl and laureth sulphates, petroleum products, phthalates, parabens and fragrances that are listed. (If you see a fragrance listed by name – limonene, for instance – it's because it has been shown to cause irritation in some users, so avoid!)

Opt for products, including wet wipes, which don't contain any of the above. CSJK9, Ekoneem, Pet Head, etc., all make great products. You'll find them all in my shop www.myitchydog.co.uk along with bags of information. Read the label carefully. As a rule of thumb, when buying online, if the ingredients aren't listed, shop elsewhere.

Air fresheners

In a recent study on the toxic effects of air freshener emissions*, scientists wanted to test whether or not commercial air fresheners caused acute toxic effects in mammals. The short answer is yes. It showed that actually, instead of clearing the air of pollutants it just adds to them. Further studies have shown that mammals who are at home a lot – pregnant women, new mothers, babies and pets – suffer more depression, wheezing, diarrhoea and skin problems as a result of the volatile organic compounds contained in air fresheners. The best treatment? Ditch the air, carpet and furniture fresheners. It's really that simple. Air fresheners have been linked to sick building syndrome and sleep disturbances, too. Get rid.

*Anderson RC, Anderson JH, published in the *Archives of Environmental Health* 1997

Other reasons for problem skin

Secondary infections

It's hard enough getting a child to stop scratching when they're super-itchy – with chicken pox, for instance. It's nigh on impossible to get a dog to quit. And if she sleeps in your room at night she's probably going to be responsible for a fair few heated words hissed into the darkness, followed by a crisis management bacon sandwich before work.

If dogs are scratching with dirty claws, nibbling and licking at skin damage or rubbing their itchy parts across the carpet, it's hardly surprising that some will get a secondary bacterial infection, and no one wants to have to resort to the Cone of Shame to stop it. Luckily it is easy to treat small areas of secondary infection, and just as easy to avoid getting one by controlling the initial itching problem.

Treatment:
Neem oil

Ekoneem is great, applied directly to the infected area, twice a day. It should sort out all but the most prolific of skin infections. For infection in larger areas: wash your dog with a good neem shampoo in which neem is the very first ingredient followed by essential oils that reduce inflammation – sage and rosemary oils are great. Try CSJK9's Skinny Shampoo. Give her a good shampoo then apply the neem oil to the worst parts a couple of times a day until sorted.

The key here is not to let the scratching get out of control to such an extent that only a trip to the vet and a course of antibiotics will clear it up.

Poor diet

Too many overprocessed carbohydrates and sugars in your dog's diet can lead to an overgrowth of *Candida albicans*, a yeast that lives happily in the gut and on skin. When the carbs have stressed your dog's gut to the max the *Candida* becomes irritated – in the gut, up the nose, in the ears and on the skin's surface. It's extremely itchy but not hard to get rid of.

Treatment:
A short-term probiotic
A change in diet

Something like Yumpro, from Lintbells, will do the trick and get the gut flora back on an even keel. Move your dog over to a better food, possibly one that's grain-free to cut down on the carbs and sugars. Do the same for treats too.

Stress or boredom

Stress can be a short-term problem that causes dogs to scratch more, around big events, and it can be coupled with boredom when they're left home alone, especially if they are of a breed prone to separation anxiety.

Treatment:
For boredom: interactive dog toys and puzzles are great, especially if they make the dog work out a problem in order to get food.

Try Nina Ottosson www.nina-ottosson.com for the best interactive toys on the market.

Make him work for breakfast. Either use one of the toys above or give him a Kong which you made earlier – i.e. which has been stuffed with his breakfast and then frozen. A Kong is a very hard rubber toy that comes in various shapes, sizes and colours. Each toy has a hole in the bottom into which you can put food or treats for the dog to work at retrieving. Give him a frozen Kong for breakfast as you leave for work. Not only will that pass a couple of hours but your dog will associate you leaving the house with food arriving.

For stress: try Dorwest Scullcap and Valerian tablets, especially around key events – fireworks, travelling, when you have lots of guests over – Christmas, for instance. Also, dead simple, leave a radio playing quietly near to where your dog spends most of his day. Either way, if you think your dog's scratching is due to being left alone for long periods, you will need to try and sort that out: if you can't arrange to be at home more, invest in a good dog walker.

Less likely causes:

Genetics – breed-specific itching – particularly susceptible are German shepherds, West Highland white terriers, retrievers, Dalmatians, shih-tzus, boxers, poodles, English bulldogs, bull terriers, beagles and Boston terriers

Autoimmune disorders, such as lupus. Very rare

Metabolic and hormonal disorders

Perfect
paws

A note on probiotics

Please don't give your dog a probiotic made for humans. I had a customer call recently to say she was giving her dog a well-known drink containing lots of 'good bacteria'. She wanted to know if it would help her dog's digestive 'issues'. I had to say that it probably wouldn't. Mainly because it contains not one, but three types of sugar. A dog's gut doesn't like sugar; it's one of the biggest culprits in causing an upset stomach, leading to the problems that the 'good bacteria' are meant to sort out. Even for us humans, your average probiotic drink is probably one of the most counter-intuitive food products I've ever come across. Don't waste your money.

Whichever probiotic you're thinking of giving, take a really good look at the label first. I just read the ingredients list of one particular probiotic made for dogs: the first ingredient was meat and animal derivatives. If you're trying to improve your dog's gut health, this isn't what you need to see. The first ingredients you want to see are prebiotic and probiotic.

HOW TO AVOID SKIN PROBLEMS

Give your dog a calm environment

Don't leave him alone all day

Brush your dog regularly

Feed him the best food you can

Keep on top of fleas and worms

Clean and vacuum regularly

Use good-quality shampoo

GROOMING PRODUCT INGREDIENTS TO AVOID

Sodium lauryl sulphate

Sodium laureth sulphate

Parabens

Phthalates

D-Limonene and any other fragrance listed separately

GROOMING PRODUCT INGREDIENTS TO EMBRACE

Oats or oatmeal – it's not just for flapjacks

Coconut – very soothing

Neem – a natural insect repellent, antifungal, antibacterial

Essential oils – sage and rosemary

Glycerine – a simple product for holding it all together

REMEDIES FOR SKIN CONDITIONS

Pure organic neem oil

A neem-based shampoo
with essential oils

Ekoneem shampoo bar

Neem and coconut cream

Dermacton

SUPPLEMENTS FOR SKIN CONDITIONS

A good omega 3, 6 and 9 fish
and plant oil supplement
(see pages 176-7 for more on that)

Echinacea

Coconut oil

Probiotics

A herbal flea, tick and mite mix

A herbal wormer

'Thith tathes awethome'

Skin problem checklist

Like so many diseases that present with 'flu-like symptoms' in humans, dogs can itch for all sorts of reasons. See if any of the possible symptoms listed below can give you a clue to what ails your dog.

Itchy skin all over – could be anything – food, mites, pollens

Itching at the base of the tail and down the back – possibly fleas, worms or blocked anal glands

Chewing at the top of their back legs – blocked anal glands, worms or fleas, reaction to whatever they've been rubbing themselves against: trees maybe

Itchy paws, being chewed and licked constantly, often resulting in brown staining of the fur – house dust mites, harvest mites, grass seeds or *Candida* overgrowth

Itchy, red and sore belly, groin and armpits – bites, contact allergy to grass, sarcoptic mange

Itchy face, especially with fur loss around the eyes – demodectic mange, or simply sticking their faces into plants which don't agree with them

Itchy paw pads – house dust mites, harvest mites, a sensitivity to cleaning products, or *Candida*

Itchy, gunky, smelly, red ears, with lots of head shaking – ear mites, harvest mites, *Candida*

Circular patches – ringworm (which is actually a fungal condition)

Little red spots on the skin – allergies or folliculitis (mild bacterial infection), secondary probably to another condition, maybe mange

Little raised lumps under the skin – *Candida*, malassezia (more fungal loveliness), heat rash

Itchy, runny eyes, runny nose, wheezing, sneezing or coughing – hay fever

Smelly skin – *Candida*, seborrhea (you'll also have greasy, scaly skin for this one)

Hair loss, more shedding than usual – stress, environment, central heating, a poor diet

Greasy, scaly skin – seborrhea due to allergies or hormonal imbalance

Skin colour or texture changes – an untreated long-term skin problem or hormonal changes – talk to your vet

Itchy, raw patch on fore leg, or lick granuloma caused by excessive licking – could actually be that your dog is in pain – check with vet

Red, irritated patches of raw skin, probably a hot spot – could be allergies, bites or the result of chewing and licking that spot

Just one or many of these symptoms could be going on at once. Have a chat with your vet to make sure there's nothing more sinister underlying the itching, then you can get on with treating it as naturally as possible. It may never go away; it may be a case of managing the problem. Just remember that these symptoms are the immune system's response to something it sees as an invader, so long-term steroids will only mask the problem, rather than solve it, and long-term antibiotics will weaken the immune system further.

❧ An upset ❧ stomach/gastritis / diarrhoea

The canine gastrointestinal tract is the shortest digestive system among mammals, with a plate to poo time of around 8-9 hours in an adult dog. Unlike us humans, whose digestion processes start in the mouth as we chew, the enzymes in our saliva setting to work on our food while it can still see daylight, dogs only start to process their food once it's landed in their stomachs.

A dog's stomach contains a lot of hydrochloric acid, which it uses to process lumps of protein and bone, turning this into a liquid before passing it on to the small intestine. Dogs also have a strong regurgitation reflex (peristalsis), allowing them to throw back up food which is too big for them to handle. It can then be re-eaten and swallowed in smaller, more manageable pieces. Grim, but handy! High stomach acidity is also the reason dogs can eat three-day-old pizza and not spend days wondering which end they should point at the loo first, like we would.

The small intestine is where the main digestion takes place. This is

where the nutrients from the food are passed through the intestine walls, into the body and off to wherever they're needed. Once in the large intestine, the last vitamins and minerals are passed into the body before any waste matter is excreted and left for you to pick up, you lucky thing.

The digestive pipeline

Think of your dog's digestion as a pipeline. Food, treats, water, supplements, drugs, bits of paper and glitter (or whatever your dog's proclivity is for banned substances) go in one end, and numbers 1 and 2 come out the other.

What goes in is reflected not only in what comes out the rear end – wind, diarrhoea, that gelatinous, bloody horror show known as colitis – but also in what shows up on the outside: smelly skin, gunky eyes and ears, blocked anal glands, greasy fur. All this is partly a reflection of the health of your dog's gut, and changing to the right diet can work wonders to improve things.

Common problems caused by poor diet

Wind/flatulence
Bad breath
Candida (yeast overgrowth)
Loose stools
Poor coat condition
That classic doggie smell

Allergies
Itchy skin
Blocked anal glands
Constipation
Lack of energy and concentration
Too much of that twitchy energy

Just about everything on the list above can be fixed with a change of diet and a good short-term supplement. Which supplement depends on what the problem is (for a full run-down on canine food supplements, see p171).

Wind, bad breath, *Candida*, loose stools, poor coat condition and that doggie smell

Treatment:
Prebiotic
Probiotic
Keepers Mix

If I had a dog with any, or all, of this little lot I would use a short-term mixture of these three supplements. I'd also change them to a different food for a while to see if that was the cause, and keep the carbs down too. To get the prebiotic and probiotic in, try a product like Bionic Biotic from Pooch & Mutt or Yumpro from Lintbells. I would also recommend moving onto Feelwells probiotic dog treats. One month on a bag of those bad boys and you can stand down from fart duty.

For getting your dog's general condition back, I'd put them onto Dorwest Keepers Mix, certainly for a few months and, if you stop using it and the problems return, put them on it for good. Keepers Mix is a blend of kelp, celery seeds, alfalfa, nettles, rosemary, psyllium husks, clivers and wild yam. It can be taken alongside any medication and each herb works on a different part of your dog: rosemary for digestion and wind, psyllium for bowel health and digestion and wild yam to maintain healthy intestines. Keepers Mix is all round a very good thing indeed.

Constipation, lack of energy and concentration, too much of that twitchy energy

Treatment:
A change of diet
Better exercise

As long as you've had the vet check your dog over to make sure there are no underlying problems, I'd look at changing her to a food with better ingredients and less carbohydrate, especially reducing the overprocessed kind which really plays havoc with her blood sugars. A better source of fibre, from vegetables, for instance, will help with constipation and anal gland problems.

Also, lack of movement can lead to dogs being constipated, just as it can with us, and if your dog's stools are either too loose or too hard, she may develop blocked anal glands (see p152). Constipation really saps the energy too.

Enteritis and gastritis

If your vet has diagnosed enteritis or gastritis your dog has either inflammation of the gastrointestinal tract (enteritis) or an inflammation of the lining of the stomach (gastritis) which can be caused by all sorts – anything from a dodgy scavenging session to parvovirus, or an intestinal blockage. Once your dog has received a thorough check-over and anything sinister has been ruled out, the vet may prescribe an anti-nausea drug or a painkiller; after that, it's either a couple of days of starving your dog or feeding her on only simple food – fish and rice, for instance – and making sure there is always plenty of fresh water to drink. Because, let's face it, there's going to be a lot of runny stuff coming out of one or both ends, which can dehydrate a dog very quickly. Let her take it easy; leave her in peace to recuperate and exercise her only as and when she feels she's up to it.

Changing to raw feeding for general gut health

I'm not going to come over all raw feeding on you now. It certainly doesn't always agree with Nikita. One batch of frozen raw food I tried her on resulted in

✿ A dental ✿ problem

Writing this book has changed the way I prioritise Nikita's needs over her wants. Mostly she 'wants' her dinner. And my dinner. And the cat's dinner. What she 'needs' are healthy teeth and gums, which she'll sadly never have. Nikita's teeth and gums are shocking. You've heard the term 'dog breath' – well, her breath knows no bounds, and that's down to the state of her poor old gnashers and gums.

It's just unfortunate that when Nikita was found on the street her teeth were already in an irreversibly awful state. So bad, in fact, the vet thought she was much older than she is. After a good clean, her age was amended to six or seven years old, but you could see that most of the enamel on her teeth had eroded away, from a poor early start and a lifetime of neglect. So I really need to keep on top of her oral health. The problem is that I like putting my fingers in her mouth about as much as she likes having them there. Which is not at all. But if I don't do it, the vet has already told me she will start to lose her top teeth fairly soon. And Nikita has her standards; she doesn't want to look like a pucker-mouthed old lady until she actually is one, and probably not even then.

Because oral health is often overlooked, or avoided because of its prominence on the icky scale, more then 70% of dogs in the UK don't have any oral routine at all and 80% have signs of gum disease by the

the worst dog breath I'd ever encountered: it was too rich for her gut. I noticed it when we got into the car – we had to drive (quickly) to the beach with the windows fully down. The next day I changed back to her old (tinned + cooked) food and she was as right as rain.

Changing over to raw food can help, but it's not the only answer. Much more important is that, whatever you give your dog, you make it good – raw, wet, canned, dry, baked, bagged – I don't care. With dog food, more is less. The more good ingredients going in that can be easily digested by your dog, the less you have to clear up. It really is true. Try it.

age of three. Have you any idea how much poor dental health is worth to the veterinary industry?

Repent at leisure

If you think that getting a tooth-cleaning routine going will be just another expense you can do without, let's look at the cost benefit of not keeping on top of dental health.

Say a toothbrush and paste costs approximately £30 per year, over the 12-year life of an average dog that's a total of £360. Then let's say she has three dentals instead, under sedation at a cost of around £300 each (nope, not kidding) . That's £900 in dentals over 12 years. Nearly three times the cost. Not to mention the sedation risk itself. Or how about a well-known dental chew once a day? That will set you back nearly £1200 at today's prices.

Dogs are double 'ard!

It's not always easy to spot a dog with a dental problem. A dog won't come to you pointing at his mouth; he's more likely to spend a lot of time licking his paw or foreleg to help with the pain, or dribbling into his bedding. This happened to my friend Helen's Border terrier. She asked me what I could recommend as Lola was licking one spot on her leg so much her fur was disappearing. On taking her to the vet the next day, she discovered Lola had a broken tooth, not a skin problem. She had kept her discomfort hidden, by licking. Lola's hardcore, but by no means unusual.

Treatment:
Seaweed and parsley supplement
Hard chews and raw bones
Regular teeth brushing

Let's start with the easy fix. I haven't mentioned seaweed much before now but this is the place to start for sure. A seaweed supplement, added daily to food, will break down tartar and plaque. It can take anything up to a couple of months to see a big difference but it's well worth doing. As it's a supplement, it works systemically, not locally, on the teeth and gums. Compounds in seaweed kill the bacteria which cause plaque. Over time it will also whittle away at tartar, which falls away from the teeth and gets swallowed, another grim fact you didn't need.

It has made a massive difference to Nikita's breath! And it's kept her teeth clean too. Not only that but it's the cheapest method by far. A collie, for instance, would get through about £15-worth a year.

The only two caveats to this are – if your dog has a lot of tartar it may be best to get her teeth cleaned first by the vet then start afresh; and, because of the iodine content in seaweed, it's not suitable for dogs or cats with hyperthyroidism (this mostly affects older cats, but dogs can suffer too). I recommend CSJ's Seaweed & Parsley or ProDen Plaque Off.

Hard chews containing compounds to fight bacteria aren't my favourite thing, mostly because they list meat and animal derivatives in the ingredients and I'm not happy giving something to the dog if I don't know what's in it. If you find one that lists lovely ingredients and a plaque-fighting addition please email me because I'll stock it immediately!

Nothing wrong, though, with getting a good chewing action going for cleaning teeth. There are some good dog chews called Whimzees, which are gluten-free and vegetable-based. The thing I like about them is that they list the ingredients in full, not in categories, so you know what you're getting. Great for dogs who need to watch what they're eating.

As for bones, the only time I've ever come across dogs with sparkling teeth is when they're fed a raw diet. It's the bones that do it. All that chewing action and no cack left on the teeth that they get from eating wet or dry food.

Bones are brill for cleaning your dog's teeth, but a broken or fractured tooth will cost you a small fortune at the vet's and not inconsiderable pain to your dog. So I would avoid bones too big for your dog to handle. I get a tray of marrowbones from the butcher for a couple of pounds. If they're too small I don't bother because they're a choking hazard. If they're too big he saws them in half for me. They have a little meat on them and Nikita spends a good hour carving the marrow out with her teeth. She loves it.

Always feed bones raw, never cooked, and keep an eye on your dog. It's said that chicken bones are too soft to make a difference, dentally speaking, and there's probably some truth in that, but they're certainly not going to do any harm and they're a good starting point.

If you're not confident around raw bones, or don't have any outside space, try a deer antler. Made by Pure Dog (the Stag Bar) or Farm Foods (Antlers) are pure deer antler, which won't splinter. They take months to wear down, don't smell or get sticky and won't stain your carpet.

And, finally, on to regular brushing. I'm afraid so. Common dental problems in dogs start with plaque, which leads to bad breath and inflammation of the gums (gingivitis). Over time this inflammation works its way down into the bone and tooth loss follows. The minute the dog eats, plaque starts to build up. If you don't brush their teeth, plaque turns to tartar. Plaque can be brushed away, but tartar has to be scraped off. Under sedation.

Brushing won't be well received the first time you try it, nor the second, but it's something to persevere with. In the long run it will save your dog a lot of pain, by way of infection, sore gums and lost teeth. On a more serious note we know from studies that tooth decay and gum disease can lead to far more serious problems with major organs – heart, liver and kidneys – as bacteria from the gums leak out into the system.

How to clean a dog's teeth

Start slowly, act casual, don't make it into a big deal. That's my advice. Get yourself either a tooth-cleaning cloth or a toothbrush, from the vet or pet shop. Toothbrushes made for dogs tend to have a longer handle and two heads, one at each end, in two sizes for bigger or smaller mouths. At the same time, pick up a tube of toothpaste specifically for dogs. It comes in all sorts of flavours – including chicken and beef. Dorwest make Roast Dinner toothpaste.

REALLY IMPORTANT – don't ever use human toothpaste on your dog. Most human paste contains xylitol, a sweetener that is very toxic to dogs, and because you're not going to get the dog to rinse and spit, he's going to swallow it.

You want to put toothpaste on the cloth or brush, then gently rub it along the outside of your dog's teeth and gums; no need to do the insides too, unless he'll let you, then bravo. Your dog then takes over and spreads the toothpaste about by licking it. Job done in a minute or less.

This is how I got Nikita used to it.

Day one:
I got a tooth-cleaning cloth, a little sock for your finger, impregnated with colloidal silver, which kills bacteria. I put it on my finger and let Nikita get used to the smell, then I put little chicken-flavoured toothpaste onto the cloth and let her lick it off.

Days two and three:
I did the same again and this time I gently pushed my finger in between her gums and cheek and let her lick the toothpaste off while I gently rubbed a couple of teeth.

Days four and five:
Same again but moved my finger around the front and to the other side a little.

Day six:
This time I opened her mouth a little and brushed all her teeth but didn't push right to the back.

Day seven:
I brushed all her teeth and have done ever since.

Don't give up. It's too important to neglect, and it's even worth working with a trainer if you can't get the hang of it.

Some dogs won't ever get used to having their teeth cleaned. If you do nothing else, start them on a seaweed food supplement, every day.

Lameness / arthritis

Mobility problems in dogs are generally degenerative, developmental or inherited. And then there are those self-imposed ones, caused, I like to think, by a dog's skewed sense of danger. If I turn around after washing my hands to grab a towel and a drop of water hits Nikita's skin, she thinks the world's just caved in. But if we're on a walk and there's the merest whiff of a fox, she completely loses what scant road sense she has and will try to run across a road without hesitation. Injury can mean all sorts of lasting damage to the joints, tendons and ligaments.

Think how much ground your dog covers compared to you on a walk. You're A to B and back: walk along towpath to pub/follow footpath to pub/walk along beach to café (delete as appropriate) and back. Your dog is A - Z - J - F - back to Z, ooh, squirrel! Backwards and forwards, lowering its head to sniff the ground, running at full pelt from a standing start, swerving at extremely short notice to avoid obstacles, or just smacking straight into whatever's in the way, usually you. Chasing balls, chasing people, chasing seagulls, chasing anything that moves. Your dog's joints really take a pounding.

So mobility is incredibly important to dogs and you need to look for subtle signs that there's a problem because, as we know, dogs hide pain to avoid appearing weak. If it looks like your dog is finding it hard work to get out of bed, lie down, go upstairs, or get into the car – or he's developed a rolling gait – then it's time for a check-up. Many mobility problems – whether or not they have been treated surgically – will need managing for life, through proper weight maintenance, the right amount of exercise, a good joint supplement and sometimes physical therapy.

I'm not going to discuss possible surgery, anti-inflammatories or any other type of veterinary treatment your dog may need. That's a discussion between you and your vet. I'm going to talk simply about prevention strategies, about ways of managing lameness or joint problems from your end, at home, in the long-term.

Common mobility problems

Hip dysplasia
Elbow dysplasia
Cruciate ligament injury leading to secondary arthritis
Hind limb lameness
Knee and ankle problems
Osteoarthritis
Disc herniation

Signs that your dog may have pain in their joints

Lameness – holding a limb up, avoiding bearing weight

Not running as far or as fast as she used to

Having difficulty jumping up on things she used to have no problem with

Lack of interest in the activities she used to love

Licking a particular spot, an elbow, for instance

Hip dysplasia – is the most common mobility complaint in dogs. It's not present at birth but evolves over the first few months, coming to light at between six and 12 months of age. It's where the socket and ball joint grow in a deformed way – the socket resembles a saucer while the ball joint grows with a flat top. It's most common in large or fast-growing dogs. If your dog has hip dysplasia it's almost certainly going to develop arthritis too. Joy of joys.

It's likely to affect both hips and treatment depends on the severity of the pain and how badly mobility is affected.

Elbow dysplasia – is a genetic condition in which the three bones that make up the elbow don't fit together properly. Undue pressure is consequently put onto areas of bone, causing inflammation, osteoarthritis

and degenerative injuries such as stress fractures and cartilage erosion. Surgery isn't so common, though arthroscopy (a peek inside the elbow using a tiny camera) is performed on dogs more commonly now. It's another one of those conditions for which weight management and a good supplement will go a long way to reducing pain, symptoms and inflammation of the joints.

Cruciate ligament – is a long-term degenerative injury in dogs. Our cruciate ligaments snap due to a high impact, while playing sport, for instance, whereas a dog's wear over time. The cruciate ligament is a band of fibrous tissue that attaches the thigh bone to the shin bone over the knee (there's a song in there somewhere), and it wears away, like a fraying rope. This is one of those injuries that responds very well to surgery, with a high success rate.

Osteoarthritis – degrades the fluid cushion that protects joints, along with synovial fluid, tendons, ligaments and cartilage. A good joint supplement will work to slow the degradation process and offer relief for the symptoms of osteoarthritis.

Degenerative problems – knee and ankle, hind-limb lameness and disc herniation.

'I'll be
on your
bed later'

Treatment:
Physiotherapy or hydrotherapy
Acupuncture
Weight management
A good joint supplement

Physical therapies

Only go for a physical therapy or acupuncture if it's recommended by your vet, and consult whomever they recommend. Hydrotherapy is great for building muscle to compensate for what they lose through the inability to exercise as much as they used to. Acupuncture has a sound, well-documented place in science. It is now widely believed to stimulate our own body's repair mechanisms, including the nervous system. Although acupuncture is gaining popularity among dog owners, especially to help with pain and nerve damage, it should be noted that it is illegal in the UK for anyone other than a veterinary surgeon, qualified in acupuncture, to treat animals. Ask to see their qualifications.

Joint supplements

Give them a good mobility supplement every day. I recommend Yumove by Lintbells. I'll explain why in a minute.

It will pay off in spades to do your research before you start off on a supplement, especially if it's for life. A product costing a fiver or 50 quid could contain the same poor levels of the key ingredient. So always check before you buy. Better your dog actually benefits from a supplement and doesn't just pee it out on the nearest tree. (Which reminds me, I read an article once, in the *New Scientist* so it must be true, which said that Americans have the most expensive pee, per litre, in the world due to the quantity of supplements they take. Just sayin'.)

And, as I have said earlier, READ THE LABEL. I've just been reading a few labels on tubs of joint supplements. I'm thinking, but stop me if you disagree, that chicken 'flavour', calcium carbonate and 'encapsulated fish oil' are A: vague and B: unnecessary. I want active ingredients, not flavours, fish oil of indeterminate origin and what is, let's face it, chalk, in my supplements.

This is what I look for in a joint supplement, and Yumove has them all:

1. Glucosamine HCI occurs naturally in the body in the thick fluid around the joints, but stores deplete as we age. Derived from sea shells, the most popular form is glucosamine sulphate, but glucosamine hydrochloride or HCI is being used more often now as it's a more concentrated form of glucosamine and contains less sodium per dose. Glucosamine helps to retain that joint fluid for as long as possible, keeping the bones apart for longer, thereby reducing wear and pain.

2. Chondroitin can be a contentious one as most chondroitin used for joint supplements is either marine (shark fin) or bovine (moo cows). Ethically, I don't have a problem with the bovine form because I eat meat and I figure it's only right we should use as much of the beast as possible, and give a silent thanks to it. Shark is a different thing altogether because they're not farmed and I don't want them caught just for their fins. So if you want to avoid chondroitin from sharks steer clear of supplements labelled marine chondroitin. Also, there is an easier way to get it... in the form of green-lipped mussel extract, which also provides omega 3 fatty acids. (Green-lipped mussels are all over the place in New Zealand, and now they're farmed extensively. I lived there for a while in the late 90s and you could collect them at low tide or pick up a bag fresh from the tank for around 15p a kilo – no, it's not a typo – in any supermarket. Delicious and very good for you if you don't count the hot chips and freezing cold beer that come with them.)

3. Manganese is an essential trace nutrient found in bones and connective tissue.

4. Hyaluronic acid is the main component of synovial fluid which acts as a lubricant in the synovial joints, reducing friction between cartilage and joints.

Put all these together and you have a supplement that lubricates joints, slows wear and tear, helps to repair ligaments, reduces inflammation around cartilage and tendons and keeps fluid between the joints gooey and viscous as possible for as long as possible. All this allows for increased mobility, reduced pain and a better life. Notice I haven't mentioned chalk or chicken flavour as a recommended ingredient.

🐾 Urinary problems 🐾

Urinary problems come in two sizes – minor and serious. If in any doubt, consult a vet. Only treat an ongoing issue naturally if you've ruled out anything serious. The advice that follows is suitable for urinary problems which are caused by old age, or ongoing issues that your vet has checked.

Urinary Incontinence

Proper urinary incontinence is when your dog pees involuntarily, usually when she lies down and in small amounts. Peeing in the house, leaving a big puddle on the floor, is far more likely to be a training issue or because she can't get outside to do it.

Urinary incontinence is much more common in older dogs, especially females and the larger, heavier breeds. The most common reason is hormone

depletion. As dogs get older their levels
of oestrogen and testosterone reduce
and one of the side-effects of that is that
their sphincter muscles and bladder
neck become weaker, leading to leakage.
Bad news for them – and us – but great
news for pad manufacturers. Urinary
incontinence can also be a result of
spaying and neutering (hormones again),
infections, kidney problems, spine and
nerve damage and neurological conditions
such as epilepsy.

Lying in your own pee is just as
distressing for dogs as it would be for us.

Not only that but urine is caustic, which
can 'burn' the skin if left on it for any
length of time. This leads to soreness,
pain and yet more distress. If you think
your dog is licking down there more than
normal or has wet fur on the back of her
legs, or generally whiffs of pee, these could
all be signs of urinary incontinence.

Helping the bladder

There are a few natural helpers you can
consider: agrimony, raspberry leaf and
mixed vegetable tablets.

Agrimony is a herb from the rose family. Its use as a treatment for incontinence has been documented as far back as the Greeks and Romans – its astringency being very effective for strengthening diminishing muscle tone in the sphincter. Add it to food daily. It can also be used to treat weakened bowel muscles.

CSJK9 produce something called Hold It! for dogs. It's pure, chopped agrimony and the feedback on it is brilliant. We're trialling BB on it at the moment as she's started having little accidents and has been diagnosed with incontinence due to her age.

Raspberry leaf tablets are more commonly used to tone the smooth muscle of the uterus before birth, but as the bladder is also a smooth muscle dog owners are increasingly using it for incontinence and are reporting good results.

Dorwest make mixed vegetable tablets; added to food, they act as a mild diuretic, so your dog can empty her bladder fully, meaning less leakage when she's asleep or lying down.

Relieving the external symptoms

Because urine is caustic, it can 'scald' your dog's skin, just as it causes nappy rash in a baby, and it's just as painful. Washing the affected areas with a flannel rinsed in warm water and apple cider vinegar will really soothe and clean the skin. And who doesn't like being washed with a warm flannel? Not in a weird way, but there's something comforting and nostalgic about it.

Pat the area dry and apply a soothing cream. Avoid baby nappy cream as it will probably contain zinc, which can be toxic if ingested. I'd stay away from anything harsh and go for a coconut cream (not the edible stuff you add to a Thai curry – keep up!) or Dermacton – that's another great one that my customers rate highly. Whatever you choose, make sure it doesn't contain steroids either. Just something nice and gentle made specifically for dogs.

Rub it in to clean skin a couple of times a day and it will really help. It will probably make you feel better, too, to know that at least you're offering relief for sore skin while you're working out what's causing the leaking.

Bedding

Invest in dog beds you can wash frequently, or line her bedding with Vetbed or another good-quality, absorbent bedding which can be washed daily. I've also known dog owners who use small, synthetic-filled duvets they can wash repeatedly.

🐾 Obesity / 🐾 weight control

Keeping the weight off your dog is key to having a healthier, livelier dog, for longer. The less timber he's carrying, the easier it is to get up the stairs and the less pressure he adds to every step. This means less pain and less wear and tear, slowing degeneration as much as possible. Keeping his weight under control also means less chance of developing diabetes, heart disease and some cancers.

Did you know that too much fat in the body leads to inflammation of the joint tissues? I blame Green & Black's, Ben & Jerry's and Pieminister (not necessarily in that order) for my fat backside, but of course the fault lies entirely with me. It's the same for your dog – it's also down to you. But what does a proper weight look like? Have a look at the chart (overleaf). I know some of you will be surprised.

Don't let the ribs scare you

A few years ago, someone reported my sister to the RSPCA, concerned that her lurcher, the lovely Bud, was being starved. The inspector took one look at Bud, turned around and left, casting a casual 'He looks like a lurcher's supposed to look' over his shoulder. What he meant is, you could clearly see his ribs. Bud wasn't a bag of bones; you couldn't you see his hips from space the way you can on a poor starved creature. He just looked proper.

A while later, at a dog show, I met a lady with greyhounds who said she liked her dogs to have some fat on them. She didn't like seeing any bones, because her perception was that visible bones in this day and age denoted neglect, and she thought it was healthier if her dog was fat. With dogs, just as with humans, we've lost perspective on what a healthy weight looks like. It's far easier to keep an eye on your dog's weight than it is on your own. Or at least it is in my case.

Don't be afraid of change

If your dog is overweight, don't be scared to have a really good look at his diet and change it if you want to. If he's been eating the same thing year after year he may well get a mild case of the squits for a couple of days, because his gut is getting used to the change, but this soon passes.

I'm going to stick my neck out and say that you don't have to listen to your vet, the pet shop, or anyone else who says that your dog must eat the same food every day, without deviation. Or that he must be given an expensive prescription-only food. Have another read of the diet section and email me – kate@myitchydog.co.uk – if you have any questions or need advice on how to go about changing your dog's diet.

It winds me up that the diet industry

Body condition scoring

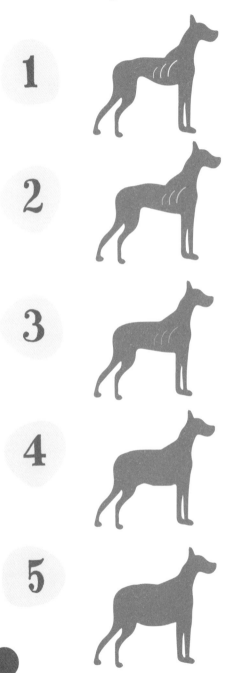

1 Ribs, spine and bony protrusions are easily seen at a distance. These pets have lost muscle mass and there is no observable body fat. **Emaciated, bony and starved in appearance.**

2 Ribs, spine and other bones are easily felt. These pets have an obvious waist when viewed from above and an abdominal tuck. **Thin, lean or skinny in appearance.**

3 Ribs and spine are easily felt but not necessarily seen. There is a waist when viewed from above and the abdomen is raised and not sagging when viewed from the side. **Normal, ideal and often muscular in appearance.**

Ideal

4 Ribs and spine are hard to feel or count underneath fat deposits. Waist is distended or often pear-shaped when viewed from above. The abdomen sags when seen from the side. There are typically fat deposits on the hips, base of tail and chest. **Overweight, heavy or stout.**

5 Large fat deposits over the chest, back, tail base and hindquarters. The abdomen sags prominently and there is no waist when viewed from above. **The chest and abdomen often appear distended or swollen. Obese.**

with its 'eat this or you're doing it wrong' mentality has seeped into our pet food industry. It's made us fearful of following our gut instincts and eroded our confidence. Change your dog's diet, get a better food, cut out calories he doesn't need and exercise him more. If you need help, just ask. Many vets run weight clinics – and do use them for their advice and support – but go your own way on food. Your dog will be happier for it and I guarantee you'll save money too.

🐾 Vaccination 🐾

To vaccinate or not to vaccinate is just as much an emotive issue for pet owners as it is among parents.

So I'll get right off the fence with this one straight away – I think vaccines are the 20th century's gift to the world and that we should avail ourselves, our children and our pets of them at every opportunity. Then I'll hop over the fence and go on to say that in the UK we over-vaccinate our pets like no one else.

Risk v reality

It seems to me that these days we want a cast-iron, 100% guarantee that something will work all the time, every time and won't ever fail. And sadly there is no such thing as a 0% failure rate. Life doesn't come with any guarantees. We have to take a risk, based on our best guess and using the information we have to hand. And, in the case of vaccines, the risk of not vaccinating far outweighs the risk of any side effect we may suffer from having it, so we should roll up our sleeves, stick our our tongues and give thanks that we have access to them at all.

That said, there's no need to overdo it. I personally will vaccinate my pets against their core diseases. I will vaccinate myself against diseases when I am travelling but I won't be vaccinating any of us on a regular basis just for the hell of it.

How vaccines work

By introducing an altered version of a disease, a vaccine triggers the body's immune response as if the body has been infected with the actual disease. If your body then meets the Real McCoy one day, your immune system will recognise it and can immediately produce the antibodies to fight it off instead of going through the whole horrible process of working out what it is first.

Core canine vaccines in the UK

Dogs need the following core vaccines:

Canine distemper virus (CDV)
Canine adenovirus (CAV)
Canine parvovirus type 2 (CPV-2)

How long does a vaccine protect my dog?

The lifetime of a vaccine, the time for which it gives you all, or partial, protection from a disease, is known as Duration of Immunity (DOI). For distemper, for instance, DOI is nine years or longer (whereas your DOI after a natural infection is lifelong, as long as it hasn't killed you in the process – pox parties my eye!).

What would one of these diseases do to my dog?

It depends on the disease, of course, but consider this before you dismiss vaccination out of hand: how ill your dog becomes and its survival depends on his general health. Dogs with a compromised immune system, who can't be vaccinated, will be at high risk of becoming infected and won't be able to fend off disease so easily. A high take-up of vaccinations among dog owners means that a herd immunity is created, protecting those that cannot be immunised. But, if you really need to know...

Canine distemper – a horrible way to go

This is the number one cause of death from infectious disease among dogs, in the world. It's a bit like the measles virus in humans and is 'shed' from infected animals through all their secretions, including tears. It attacks the cells that line the surfaces of the dog's body, including the brain. The symptoms start off with fever, move on to listlessness, discharge from eyes and nose and loss of appetite. Vomiting and diarrhoea then lead to dehydration. After a while the discharge from the nose becomes thick and sticky. Your dog starts to cough and pus blisters appear on her abdomen.

As if that wasn't bad enough, the distemper virus then gets stuck into the brain, causing encephalitis (inflammation of the lining of the brain). Your dog starts to slobber, shakes her head repeatedly and starts chewing at nothing (remember the poor, mad cows?) On it goes, ending with seizures, and possibly death.

Now, when was the last time you saw a dog doing that? I'm guessing, if you don't work in the pet primary healthcare industry, probably never. And why would you want to? It's a horrible way to go and it takes weeks. You haven't seen it because we vaccinate against it.

Puppies and maternal immunity

What mum takes away with one hand (worms!) she gives with another, the gift of temporary immunity. Puppies, like human babies, are born with a maternal immunity known as a Maternally Derived Antibodies (MDA), also known as passive immunity. Maternal antibodies interfere with vaccination efficacy, which is why you don't start a vaccination programme until puppies are 8-9 weeks old. They then receive a second vaccination 2 weeks later. These vaccinations essentially act as a jump start to try and get your puppy's body to develop an immune response of his own.

It's then recommended that dogs receive a booster at 14 months. This is to help ensure immunity in dogs who didn't respond so well to the first set of vaccines because their maternal immunity hadn't worn off sufficiently.

NB. Vaccinating in older and immune-compromised dogs and pregnant bitches should always be done under the supervision of your vet. Nikita, for instance, won't be having any more vaccinations, at the recommendation of the vets who rescued her.

Annual boosters? I don't think so

This is where I hop over to the other side of the fence. For years it's been standard practice for all dogs and cats to be revaccinated with annual booster jabs. The World Small Animal Veterinary Association (WSAVA) produced updated vaccination guidelines in 2010 advising against this practice. In summary, it states that:

We should only vaccinate with core vaccines

Then vaccinate less frequently

Core vaccine boosters should not be given any more frequently than every three years after the 12-month booster following the puppy/kitten series because the DOI is known to be many years and may be up to the lifetime of the pet.

A core vaccine is defined as a vaccine which all dogs, regardless of geographical location, should receive. Non-core vaccines are defined as being required only by those animals whose geography, environment or lifestyle puts them at risk of contracting a specific infection, e.g. rabies.

However, my first question would be this: if the DOI is nine years for the core diseases then why is it recommended that we revaccinate our dogs every three?

I don't think it's the vets' fault. Look at their dilemma. The manufacturer will advise how often their vaccines should be administered so your dog remains protected. If they stipulate every three years then what's a vet to do? Even if he or she knows your dog and the local area well, the manufacturer has stated a time period in which they guarantee protection. Would you take the risk of extending that time period with someone else's pet? I wouldn't. If the vet doesn't vaccinate your dog every three years and your dog goes on to develop one of these diseases, who're you going to sue? And what if your doggy day care or kennels won't accept your dog unless he's fully vaccinated? There go your two weeks in Ibiza.

Also, the veterinary world is changing. Practices are becoming far more business savvy, and many are now owned by very big companies who in turn are owned by very hungry shareholders. And they want their slice of the parvo pie at the end of the year. So sales targets (yes, damned sales targets) are becoming more of an issue now. If you can get a dog vaccinated every three years instead of every nine and you get 100 dogs a week sloping into your surgery, what choice does a vet have?

If your insurance company or vet insists you have annual boosters get a new vet and change your insurance provider.

Alternatives to vaccination

The British Association of Homeopathic Veterinary Surgeons (BAHVS) who are qualified in both conventional veterinary medicine and homeopathy state: 'Where there is no medical contra-indication, immunisation should be carried out in the normal way using the conventional tested and approved vaccines.'

There is no clinically proven alternative to a primary course of vaccinations – there just isn't. After the initial vaccinations and first booster it's possible to test for antibodies (a titre test) to establish if further vaccination is needed. If not, then great; carry on as normal. But don't not vaccinate in the first place.

At the risk of upsetting and offending homeopaths, and some of my own lovely customers, I no longer sell any homeopathic remedies, because I don't think homeopathy is anything more than a placebo. Having said that, there is growing, peer-reviewed evidence that the placebo effect is a very valid one and can help people to recover without treatment; that is, without the treatment they had been led to believe had taken place.

Homeopathic vaccines – nosodes – are supposed to work in the same way that a vaccine does. Except that a vaccine works by taking some of the live virus, distemper, for instance, chopping its arms and legs off, then introducing it to the body where the body's own immune system can produce antibodies to fight it off;

TITRE TESTING

Before your dog's three-year booster is due, you may want to get an antibody test done on her to determine whether or not she needs it.

A titre test measures antibody levels in your system. How many you have determines your level of immunity to a disease. Did you ever have a BCG (TB) vaccination at school when you were in your early teens? Do you remember a couple of weeks before all lining up to have a little daisy wheel of something shot into your wrist? That was a titre test. They were measuring to see what levels of immunity you had to TB. If you had good immunity you didn't need the BCG vaccination.

Vets are starting to get switched on to offering titre testing – my vet, for instance, charges £70 to do it.

Simple titres, for distemper and parvo, can be done while you wait, if your vet is set up to do them, otherwise the tests have to go off to the lab to be done. For rabies it's probably going to get sent off too and will cost more. But if you're not in a rabies area and you don't intend to travel to one with your dog it's not something you need to worry about.

while a nosode works by taking a tiny amount of a disease from diseased tissue – secretions, excretions and discharges – diluting it down to something so small as to often be undetectable, and then administering it to the patient's body, where it supposedly triggers an immune response to produce antibodies and fight the infection. Problem is, this is not a regulated industry so you have no way of knowing if the material was safe, if it was infected with any other diseased material and what effect it will have on the body once introduced.

The response I hear time and again is 'my dog got better with homeopathy, and he can't tell whether or not it's a placebo he's taking or not.' I say, he got better on his own, and because of all the extra care taken with him, from you and your vet (homeopathic or not).

Vaccines have almost wiped out some horrific diseases in humans and animals so that we have forgotten how horrible, debilitating and lethal they can be. If homeopathy was so good as a method of immunising us and our pets we would have been doing it for a long time before vaccines came along.

My only advice to you is that if you are considering using nosodes as an alternative to vaccination for your pets, please get their core vaccines done first and then see a homeopathic vet for follow-ups. Don't buy nosodes off the internet, ask your vet who makes up their preparations, assuming they don't do it themselves.

So, to vaccinate or not to vaccinate

Whatever you think, whatever your beliefs around your own health, not vaccinating your pet is really no option at all. At the very least your pet needs her first round of vaccines. If money is very tight just get her vaccinations done when she's a puppy when it shouldn't clash with any passive immunity she will have inherited from her mother. And there are schemes out there to help with the cost.

Look on the Dogs Trust, PDSA, Blue Cross and RSPCA websites for details. Also look out for National Vaccination Month. Each year there is a vaccination amnesty where vets across the country offer good discounts on core vaccines. Go to www. nvmonline.co.uk.

If you look at the Veterinary Medicines Directorate's report on Suspected Adverse Events for 2012 you will see that there were only 259 adverse reactions reported to live vaccines in dogs. Which perhaps sounds like a lot. But when you consider how many dogs receive vaccinations in any one year it's negligible compared to the horrible suffering and loss of life we would be facing if we didn't vaccinate.

'It's true.
I'm
adorable.'

🐾 Worms! 🐾

We all attract parasites; it's just a fact of life, and some live on or in us permanently, with no ill effects – dogs, cats, horses, even humans – but that's enough about my ex.

There's very little we can do to avoid coming into contact with these little blighters. It's their job to be good at seeking out the affable host, then hopping on board with a minimum of fuss, to feed. Fleas, ticks and mites having been covered earlier – see pp 99-115 – this section is devoted exclusively to worms, which, by the way, are somewhat easier for dogs to get than fleas. All dogs need do is lick a blade of grass containing worm eggs and they're infected.

I had worms once, when I was a kid. Turned out to be a tapeworm. It's not uncommon, apparently. I was about nine and so fascinated by my new friends (they exit the body in segments, and hey kids, there was no internet back then!) I didn't tell Mum for ages. She went nuts when I told her how long it had been but the ensuing lecture still didn't dim my interest. Once she'd 'dealt' with the situation I quite missed them and was hoping my little wriggly friends would revisit but no more appeared. Just read this back to myself. I think this paragraph probably constitutes an 'overshare'. But kids have about as much sense of personal hygiene as dogs (if you exclude the bum-sniffing hellos that dogs go in for), hence my anecdote.

Anyway, back to dogs! Someone told me recently that 70% of pets in the UK are never wormed. According to the British Veterinary Association there are scarcely any records kept about worm infection, with the exception of lungworm. So I suppose the question is: do we need to worm our dogs?

The short answer is yes – but not always. There are two ways you can worm your dog; with a chemical wormer or a herbal wormer (internal parasite control, as it's known in the trade). There is also something called worm-egg counting – see opposite. Bet you didn't see that coming!

Worm types

Worms come in several shapes and sizes, entering through the mouth, or passed on through blood and mother's milk, in puppies. The most common types of parasitic worms found in dogs in the UK are roundworms (the *Toxocara* roundworm being the most common type by far) and tapeworms. Roundworms are white and can grow to several centimetres in length, resembling bits of string, whereas tapeworms are flat, like segmented linguini. If you think you've lost your appetite now, read on. You'll never look at pasta the same way after I've finished... Tapeworms can grow to 50cm long. Both tapeworms and roundworms live in the intestines and have been known to share space with a couple of other creatures: hookworm and whipworm, though these are not nearly as prevalent in dogs in the UK. Lungworm is also found in this country and incidences of infestation are on the increase. Undetected and untreated lungworm can be fatal, hence the monitoring.

Worms need your dog!

You really couldn't make this stuff up – it's like a horror film. Worm eggs in faeces, or soil, need to be eaten by a dog or cat to develop into larvae and more worms. They then live in the intestines of your dog, passing out millions of eggs in yet more faeces, which get ingested by another animal, so the whole process can start all over again. Tapeworms hang onto the intestinal wall by the head, releasing segments packed with eggs which pass out through the faeces. These segments resemble grains of rice and will wriggle for a bit before drying out.

Signs that worms are present

They're easy to spot in puppies, as they are so small. They'll either vomit or pass roundworms – which look like string. In adult dogs more subtle signs can include weight loss, dry, coarse fur, diarrhoea, weakness, increased appetite and more bottom licking than usual (as if that were possible!).

If you don't want to treat your dog for worms just for the sake of it, go for a worm-egg count. As I can't see Worm Egg Counting for Beginners taking off, certainly not when there's Netflix, I would recommend that you do a worm-egg count by post. Yep, you can send poo by post. Just order a kit from www.wormcount.com. Follow the instructions, put it back in the post and the results will come back to you in a few days. Then you'll know whether you need to worm or not.

Lungworm – a special mention

Lungworm is on the increase in the UK and it's a nasty infection to have. It's an insidious parasite which can be fatal if left to its own devices and, when I explain how it works, it will make your skin crawl.

Your dog can pick up lungworm from eating or licking slugs, snails and frogs. Or from licking snail trails containing eggs on paths or grass. Foxes can also harbour lungworm, excreting larvae in their poo as they go, which as we all know dogs just love to roll about in. If a snail has been in your dog's drinking water or a supply of water in the garden – a neglected plant tray or a water feature, for example – lungworm can get in that way too. Foxes don't bury their poo but leave it, placed strategically in order to mark their territory. Usually outside my back door!

The lungworm travelator

You know when you're heading for your departure gate at the airport and you come to that long walkway that has a moving travelator in the middle? Now, are you going to be a lazy sod and jump on the travelator or are you going to get your last bit of exercise before you submit to hours of sedentary 'activity' on the plane? Stick with it, there is a point to this.

If you are a lungworm in this scenario, the travelator – your path to nirvana – is the lungs. I guess that makes your dog the North Terminal at Gatwick, pushing this analogy too far perhaps, but this is serious, so I tell it as a story to stick in your head.

Your dog eats or licks a slug and ingests lungworm larvae as a result. Your dog is now infected and the larvae have started their journey along the travelator. The larvae move to the gut where they penetrate the gut wall and enter the blood stream. Eventually they reach the right side of your dog's heart where they become adult worms.

Here they release eggs which hatch in the blood. The eggs then make their way to the lungs, rupturing the lung wall, entering the alveoli (the tiny air pockets in the lungs) and work their way up until they reach the top of the lungs. This makes the dog cough, bringing up the lungworms into his throat. He then swallows them and they pass through his digestive tract to exit the body in faeces so the whole process can start all over again. And that, my friends, is how the lungworm travelator works. You're cleared for take-off, doors to automatic. Have a nice flight.

How to prevent and treat lungworm

Luckily for us there is no known resistance to lungworm treatments yet, so your dog doesn't have to suffer. It's estimated that 2-6% of dogs are healthy but infected with lungworm, making them asymptomatic carriers. If you suspect your dog has lungworm take him to the vet, asap. You can also do a worm-egg count specifically for lungworm to establish the need to worm or not at www.wormcount.com for about £8.

You can treat your dog for lungworm in one of two ways – conventionally, with Advocate (UK name), or herbally, with Verm-X. If you want to treat him herbally then you MUST overlap a conventional Advocate treatment with the Verm-X. Simply administer a conventional lungworm treatment as normal and start on Verm-X at the same time. Verm-X can only eliminate any eggs or larvae that are still in the gut. It doesn't eliminate any parasite that has already left the gut and is elsewhere in the body. By overlapping the treatments you get rid of what's there and allow the Verm-X to take over. After that you can use Verm-X and worm-egg counting permanently to control lungworm.

That's enough about lungworm for me, I don't know about you.

Why it's vital to worm mums and puppies

Puppies and breeding bitches definitely need worming. Breeding bitches should be wormed before and after giving birth, from day 40 of pregnancy to two days after whelping. Panacur is the only licensed wormer for this treatment in the UK.

Puppies need to be wormed every two weeks until they're 12 weeks old because they get roundworm while in the mother's womb, through the placenta. Worms are also passed down through their mother's milk. So you might not think puppies need worming as they haven't ventured out yet, but the worms are right there, and mum is the culprit. For more information on this, see p158.

The golden rule is: don't skimp on worming treatments. Get a good one, spend the money, make sure your dog is clear of parasites. This rule applies to conventional as well as herbal parasite control. Get something that does what it says on the tin – from your vet, or buy what they would recommend, online. Or go herbal with a good product like Verm-X or Four Seasons.

Do a worm-egg count three times a year and you might not need to worm at all. The money you spend on parasite control will pay for itself in spades.

 **☙ Diabetes ☙**

I know I said at the beginning of the book that I wouldn't be commenting on serious diseases like diabetes, but as it's on the top 10 list of reasons for visiting the vet I thought it needed a mention and a bit of practical advice at least.

And it's this:

Work with your vet. A diabetic dog can live a good life but only after you've established a proper routine between the two of you. You will need to get to grips with monitoring your dog's blood sugars, feeding him at regular intervals (a recommended diet) and administering insulin. Once you've got your head around that little lot, things should start to smooth out.

Because you dog will most likely be a type 1 diabetic you're going to be looking at a lifetime of treatment. You need to make sure that the pet insurance you have covers your dog for the duration of the condition, not just for the first 12 months, which a lot of pet insurance companies do nowadays. If you consider the annual treatment for a Jack Russell can easily be £600, it's not a cheap disease.

According to a paper published in 2004 in the *Journal of Nutrition* * – 28% of dogs who develop pancreatitis go on to develop type 1 diabetes. And, of the dogs monitored for type 1, over 40% of them have

---

* Rand, JS et al, Canine and Feline Diabetes Mellitus: Nature or Nurture?

some type of pancreatic damage. As we know, pancreatitis in dogs can be caused by eating lots of fatty foods, so that's something very much in your control: avoid too much fat and keep your dog at a good weight. This can cut down the risk substantially.

🐾 Other 🐾 charming conditions

Anal glands

I swear this book gets classier the more I write. Now we're onto anal glands. Does it get any better?

Anal glands are a pair of sacs that sit one each side of a dog's anus. Also known as scent glands, every time your dog goes for a poo, liquid from the sacs is pushed out, adding your dog's scent, marking his turf. The glands get blocked quite easily, and since our dogs getting less exercise outside the home and commercial dog foods lack sufficient 'bulk' it's becoming more of a problem. We all have anal glands, yes, even you. I think it's only sea otters that don't. No idea why that is, but all other mammals have them.

Signs anal glands might be blocked

If your dog is 'scooting' across the floor on his bottom it's not likely to be worms, more blocked glands. I know it looks amusing but it's probably causing quite

a bit of discomfort if it's got to this stage. Other ways dogs try to get relief is by licking or biting around that area, and chasing their tails. Also funny to watch.

I'm not going to advise you how to unblock them, it's pretty simple but I'd never do it – I don't know precisely what I'm doing and a vet once told me it's the worst smell in the world. So it's best done by a groomer or your vet. Even better is to avoid a blockage in the first place.

Your dog's five a day

Essentially, you want to be getting a firm poo out of your dog. I sound like Gillian McKeith now! I'm not going to make you present it to me in a plastic container; honestly, I don't need to see it. A good firm poo is what you need to allow the anal sacs to empty. A soft poo won't cut the mustard. Full sacs left untreated can get infected, and may burst, causing an abscess. And small though they are, if anal sacs need removing the consequence can be incontinence. All for the want of a firm stool.

So, if your dog is on a food that agrees with him but his stools could do with a bit of firming up, add fibre. Left to their own devices, dogs eat all sorts of stuff that gives them bulk they don't digest: bone, paper, bits of whatever they come across in the gutter (disgusting creatures).

Add raw bone, whole oats or veg to your dog's dinner. Oats are good for the gut, and coat, but the dog doesn't digest them all; the same goes for vegetable fibres. Raw bones are fine either ground or as part of a carcass (make sure they're raw). So there's your bulk right there, firming up the poo, adding good nutrition to your dog's food and saving him from a painful, humiliating outing to the vet.

Eye problems

Eyes are not to be trifled with. I always get the dog or cat checked out at the vet if it's for anything other than general maintenance and cleaning. So in this section I talk briefly about common eye problems and then natural ways to maintain good eye health, plus some easy first-aid fixes. Other than that I'm standing well clear of treating scratched corneas, as should all of us.

Some breeds are more prone to certain diseases than others. For example, basset hounds, Great Danes and cocker spaniels are susceptible to glaucoma, and West Highland white terriers, Yorkshire terriers and Cavalier King Charles spaniels to conjunctivitis.

Eye problems can occur in utero, in puppies, as a result of injury or infection, poor nutrition or old age so it's always good to get any changes to your dog's eyes checked out immediately. Problems occurring inside the eye or under the eyelid fall under the radar, so what looks like a minor irritation

could be causing a lot of damage, and you don't want that going undetected. Dogs may have dry or watery eyes, rub their eyes with their forelegs, scratch them with their claws – adding bacteria to the mix – or shy away from bright light.

Causes can be a scratched cornea, cysts, conjunctivitis, an infection of the third eyelid, glaucoma, cataracts, retinal detachment – you get the idea. It's nothing you're going to be able to diagnose on your own.

Watery eyes

Nikita often gets itchy, watery eyes. Especially if we've been out on the Downs for the afternoon. It's probably all the pollen and dust swirling about. She's barely two feet off the ground after all. If I leave them she'll start licking her forelegs and using them to rub her eyes. Lord knows what bacteria lurks in that mouth.

So I use a colloidal silver spray (Lintbells Silvercare) to wipe her eyes clean and over-the-counter eye drops with added antihistamine from the optician. The vet recommended the latter to me. It really helps.

Dry eyes

Our dog BB was born with only one tear duct so one of her eyes is constantly dry and collects debris which she can't get rid of through normal tear action. We clean it using false tears, recommended by the vet but purchased from the optician. It seems to work and doesn't bother her at all.

Tear staining

There are small holes called puncta near the eye which drain tears away and down the throat. If the eye gets too irritated – from an ingrown hair or a turned-in eyelid, for instance – these can get blocked, leading to more tears spilling out, which in turn leads to staining.

Tear staining is much more noticeable in fair-furred breeds such as West Highland white terriers. Again, colloidal silver used daily to remove tears from fur will reduce the staining until it's gone completely.

There's not a lot more I can say about eye care really, in a DIY sense at least, because so much can be happening around and inside the eye that we can't see or diagnose. The only thing to add is that, again, good nutrition goes a long way to keeping your dog's eyes in good health. If it's more than daily care you're worried about, then please do go and see your vet.

Poor condition as a result of long-term illness or antibiotic/steroid use

What's that saying about the first sign of insanity being repeating the same process over and over and expecting a different result? I cannot tell you how many people I've spoken to whose dogs have been prescribed steroids and antibiotics over, and over again, with no good result. Now both most certainly have their place and can do wonders, but longer term use isn't ideal and they really effect the gut and – all together now – the health of your dog.

My questions to the vet would be: if there's no bacterial infection why prescribe antibiotics? And if there is no inflammation, or they didn't work the first time, why re-prescribe steroids?

Side effects of steroids can be:

Irritation of the stomach lining

Stomach ulcers

Fluid retention from a water and salt imbalance

Propensity to infection and delayed healing

Side-effects of antibiotics can be:

A stomach upset

A reduction of good bacteria

Thrush

A few years ago I went through a few rounds of vet visits with Pearl the cat. She was constantly pulling her fur out, itching and scratching. I felt so guilty. Her back was covered with scabs where she nibbled at the skin constantly. She didn't have fleas, and there were no other cats getting into the house to

'I'm ready
for my
blanket
now.'

wind her up. Now Pearl is a really furry cat. She's got the look of a Maine Coon, trapped in the body of a moggy. So her back resembled a bad comb-over and she was clearly miserable. These break-outs would happen a couple of times a year and last for weeks at a time.

The first couple of trips to the vet she was prescribed steroids and antibiotics, and I just let it happen. I have no idea why I didn't question the antibiotic injection he gave her, followed by a course of tablets which I nearly lost my arms over, trying to get them into her. I just wanted to relieve her itching, but I didn't get it sorted with antibiotics and steroids. It took a change in diet and a Feliway diffuser before she stopped altogether.

I had a wisdom tooth infection about 25 years ago. My dentist prescribed antibiotics and told me to come back a week later for treatment. Well, within 24 hours I had a nice case of thrush to go with it. A buy-one-get-one-free, if you like! The tooth was starting to feel better but the antibiotics had got to work destroying the good bacteria in my gut. So my 'downstairs' was in a right old state. By the time I went back to the dentist I was sore at both ends! 'Oh yes,' said the dentist, 'most people get thrush from amoxicillin!' Charming. But I have the power of speech, opposable thumbs and money, so I could sort it out at the chemist. Dogs can't. They just feel crappy. So remember that what helps your dog can also hinder her recovery.

This is where a short course of good pre- and probiotics can really help. I would also recommend a gut-calming herbal blend, such as CSJ's Heal! Added to food, it's a blend of camomile, skullcap, mint, comfrey leaf and aniseed. It will soothe the gut while the pre- and probiotics get to work on restoring the balance of bacteria throughout. A couple of weeks on that little lot will speed recovery along no end.

Pregnancy

Whether you've decided to breed from your dog or she got knocked up when you weren't looking (teenagers, eh?) there are some very effective natural

NB. Don't just stop administering medication prescribed by your vet and switch to natural overnight. Discuss it with your vet first and work out a plan for moving over gradually, if it's appropriate for your dog's condition. And please don't rely on well meaning internet forum members as your sole advisors either. Or me, for that matter!

bits and bobs you can use to ease things along.

First of all, though, if you think your dog may be pregnant, please get her checked out by the vet asap and let him or her monitor her throughout. (The average gestation period for dogs is around 65 days. If you don't know when the deed was done, your vet will be able to have a good guess based on what he or she can feel on examining your dog's abdomen.) Please also discuss any supplements or remedies with your vet prior to use. What I write below is general guidance: your dog is unique, with her own issues and foibles, so work hand in hand with your vet during her pregnancy.

As for herbal experts I am going to recommend Dorwest, wholeheartedly. Dorwest is a family-run UK company which has been researching, developing and manufacturing herbal medicines for dogs and cats since the 1940s. It is the only company in the UK to produce any registered herbal veterinary medicines – one being raspberry leaf tablets which assist in a smooth labour. They are a font of knowledge and if you want to assist your pregnant bitch through pregnancy using herbal remedies or homeopathy I suggest they would be your best port of call – www.dorwest.com.

As with humans, a dog's pregnancy is best interfered with if and when necessary. If it ain't broke, don't fix it. Keep your dog as healthy and happy as possible, with a good diet, and provide a calm and safe environment and a private, palatial, luxuriously lined whelping box for her and the pups to get to know each other in.

Fertility

If you're planning on your dog having puppies, the pregnancy is of course more under your control, allowing you to help out by making sure the right supplements are administered to maximise your dog's fertility prior to conception.

Wheatgerm oil in capsule or liquid form can be added to your bitch's and your dog's food for a week before mating and, for the bitch, for three weeks after. Wheatgerm is a good source of vitamin E, which helps to maintain fertility. It can also help in preventing miscarriage or absorption, where the foetus is absorbed by the body and effectively disappears.

Labour

For centuries women have used raspberry leaf to ease painful periods and labour pains and aid the birth process. I like it as tea, just to cleanse my system. It's also thought to have gastrointestinal benefits and is a good thing to have handy for stomach upsets. For pregnant bitches the same is true. Dorwest's raspberry leaf tablets given during pregnancy and for a a little while after can help ease labour and move the birth process along. It's especially good for bitches who have previously experienced prolonged labour and it helps with evacuation of the placenta too.

Milk not coming in or slow

While I'm still not convinced by homeopathy, many of you swear by it, and who am I to stand in the way of easing a pregnant bitch's burden? If milk isn't coming in or is slow to start, Urtica Urens 30C is highly regarded.

Parasite control during and post pregnancy

Treating a pregnant bitch for fleas, ticks and mites during pregnancy is a tricky area. Most pharmaceutical companies don't do research into the effects on pregnant pooches so don't offer advice, leaving it up to you to decide. Which is helpful. My vet, for what it's worth, recommends not treating them at all during pregnancy, just making sure to keep their environment clean and parasite-free during that time. See the section on flea, tick and mite control for how to keep the house flea-free and check with your vet to see if the current thinking has changed.

As for worming, that's a whole different can of... sorry. Keeping worms under control when she is pregnant is crucial for your dog and her pups. If your dog has worms she can pass them on to her pups in utero and through milk after birth. If you go down the pharmaceutical worming route during this time you need the right

wormer from your vet, as many of them won't cover pregnant bitches. Panacur in the UK currently does.

Herbal worming in pregnancy

If you are going down the herbal route, and this is the way I would go, do a worm-egg count www.wormcount.com; then, assuming no lungworm eggs are present, give Verm-X either in liquid or treat form throughout her pregnancy.

If lungworm eggs are present, have a chat with the vet as Verm-X only works on eggs introduced to the gut through the mouth: it won't help on parasites which have left the gut and moved into the blood. I would still use Verm-X in tandem with any conventional treatment for lungworm, and then continue with Verm-X alone.

Parasite control and puppies

Once the puppies arrive, they will be under the vet for worming and flea treatment. They need to be wormed at two, five and eight weeks old. At three months, they can move entirely on to Verm-X at half the recommended amount and then move on to the full recommended amount at six months. With regular, clear worm-egg counts you shouldn't ever have to put them back on conventional wormers again.

As for fleas, the only herbal treatment I can recommend that I know works brilliantly is CSJ's Billy No Mates, which is suitable for puppies from eight weeks, around the same time that conventional flea treatment would start. As it needs a while to become effective in the system, I would definitely treat the puppy with a conventional flea treatment as well if fleas are present.

Fleas can be fatal

Flea infestations can kill puppies very quickly – such tiny creatures soon become dehydrated as the fleas take their blood. Though I love and advocate herbal supplements for fleas and worms, pregnancy and early puppyhood is not a time to prevaricate.

Get a plan, consult your vet, stick with it and move over to herbal supplements as soon as your pups are clear of maternal parasites.

Phantom or false pregnancy

A phantom pregnancy is when a dog displays the signs and symptoms of pregnancy without actually being pregnant. It can occur after a real pregnancy or a couple of months after a bitch has come into season. Once a bitch has a phantom pregnancy it's likely to recur every season.

IMPORTANT NOTE:

I wouldn't recommended neem for pregnant bitches, as it has contraceptive properties – although studies have shown that these are quickly reversible and it doesn't affect fertility in the long-term.

The symptoms of a phantom pregnancy are often mental as well as physical and can be very distressing for all concerned. Symptoms can include:

Restlessness
Behavioural changes
Depression
Anxiety
Loss of appetite
Lactation
Nesting
Enlargement of the mammary glands
Vomiting
Distended abdomen
Watery secretion from the mammary glands

If phantom pregnancy looks likely to be a recurring feature in your dog's life then spaying is often the best option offered by your vet, though of course this is not a small matter of delving in and tying off fallopian tubes – the uterus and ovaries are removed entirely. It's something I would try my hardest to avoid.

Herbally, again raspberry leaf tablets come into their own in substantially reducing the symptoms of phantom pregnancies or preventing them altogether. Symptoms can also be relieved with homeopathic Pulsatilla 15C and Urtica Urens 3C.

I have always found scullcap and valerian tablets, or Bach's Rescue Remedy to be brilliant at relieving anxiety in times of stress and I would definitely use one of these here.

❧ Old age ❧

Old age comes to us all in the end. Let's face it, it beats the alternative! I like getting older. I wouldn't trade my life now for my 20-year-old self's, not even the body. Well, maybe the body – size 10 is a distant memory. I wonder if it's the same for dogs?

Is an old dog capable of butt envy? Does he go all misty-eyed at the pert perambulations of a younger, more spritely version of himself, or marvel at the bendy, teenage fluidity of the flibberti-gibbet labradoodle who won't stop yapping at Every. Squirrel. In. The. Park!!!

My friend's dog, Amber, is an ancient Jack Russell who's so round she has a job getting up the road. But let her loose in the park and she's off, jollying along for all she's worth, as fast as her stumpy legs will carry her rotund little form. She loves it; she just doesn't have the stamina she once did so walks are shorter, yet no less exciting.

The general rule is, the larger the breed, the shorter the lifespan. A Great Dane's average lifespan is six to eight years whereas a Jack Russell can live for up to 16. By the time a dog reaches the age of two they're at the human equivalent of 25 years old. A dog can be said to be senior when he's in the last 25% of his average life expectancy and geriatric when he's achieved that and is living beyond it.

As with humans, we reap what we sow. The better we look after our dogs in early and midlife, the longer and healthier we can expect their old age to be.

Common causes of death

I asked my vet's practice what, in their experience, was the highest cause of death among dogs. Heart disease came back as the answer, without hesitation. Here's a list of common causes of death, showing a few breeds which have high rates of each particular disease or condition, taken from a 20-year study into canine mortality rates published in 2011 by the University of Georgia.

Heart disease – Newfoundlands, Maltese, chihuahuas, Dobermans and fox terriers
Respiratory – Bulldogs, borzois, Yorkshire terriers and Afghan hounds
Gastrointestinal – Great Danes, Akitas, Gordon setters, Shar Peis and Weimaraners

Neurological – Dachshunds, miniature dachshunds, pugs, miniature pinchers and Boston terriers

Musculoskeletal – St Bernards, Irish wolfhounds, Great Danes and greyhounds

Common issues around ageing

As your dog gets older she'll start to slow down, probably want less exercise and go grey around the muzzle. Other common signs that your dog is getting on are:

Becoming clingy or more distant

Becoming more grumpy or aggressive

Staring, wandering or calling
(Ronnie has been known to stare at
the floor for ages)

Forgetfulness (we all know what
that feels like)

Less of an appetite

Tooth loss

Loss of muscle mass

These problems are generally things you manage because they're just what comes to us all in the end. I like to see old people with old dogs; it's nice to think of them wandering into the living room, looking at each other and both wondering, 'What did I come in here for?'

The physical symptoms below can be eased through supplements and diet to make them less of an issue:

Urinary incontinence (see pp136-8)

Constipation (see p127)

Putting on weight (see pp139-41)

Stiffness in the joints (see pp132-6)

As for the other general effects of aging, there are one or two very helpful things you can do to help.

Hearing loss

My friend Heather has taught her (very grumpy) Cavalier King Charles, Max, a rudimentary form of sign language. Max wasn't always deaf but he is now he's 12. Using sign language certainly helps with his mood as he's less frustrated because he can still communicate. He also enjoys grating barnacles off rocks with his teeth but that's another story.

Anyhow, back to sign language. Your dog doesn't have a clue what you're gabbing on about, he really doesn't. He works on body language, visible cues and the tone of your voice. As his hearing wanes with age he will come to rely on your signing requests to him more and more. What you probably haven't realised, though, is how much you already use sign and body language to communicate with your hearing dog. Raise your hand for a 'sit' command, put your hand to the floor for 'down' – these are common, more formal signs. Subconsciously, I sign all the time. As I open the back door and say, 'Out you go' to Nikita, what she's seeing is me cocking my head towards the back door: that's her cue, not my 'out you go' – she doesn't speak human.

Next time your dog meets another dog in the park, watch them. Everything about them is sign language – tails wagging, ears up, or flat on their backs, submitting. It's all about the signs and body language. So keep using signs and, as they get older and start to lose their hearing, signing will save you both a lot of frustration.

Senility, anxiety and fearfulness

It happens to the best of us – and around half the dogs in the UK will display signs of senility as they get older.

If your dog is becoming senile, she's likely also to be more fearful and anxious – she may start forgetting housetraining, whining, or losing awareness of what's going on around her, while indulging in compulsive behaviour, such as excessive licking, wandering and circling – and you'll need to put some coping mechanisms in place, for both of you.

She may forget where things are, so put more water bowls about the place; then if she happens upon one she can have a drink. As much as is possible feed her at the same time each day, in the same place – stick to her routine. In the case of housetraining going out the window, get her into the habit of waking, eating and going out straight away to minimise accidents around the house. Take her out several times a day, and if there are accidents never punish your dog; remember, it's not her fault.

Stick to familiar walking routes to reduce anxiety levels to a minimum. Dogs who are getting senile can also crave physical contact and need more of it in order to feel secure, especially at night when they're trying to settle. Heather often ends up on the sofa, calming Max to sleep during the night, and he's often to be seen pacing the garden at 2am.

These are the velvet ropes that bind us to our dogs, to our pets, to our furry friends. We love and care for them, the best way we know how, to give them the best possible life.

Saying goodbye

So, there you are, you're going to get old and die and the same can be said about your dog. As I've said before, though, it sure beats the alternative.

While I was writing this book I had to make the horrible decision to have Dave, my lovely handsome cat, put to sleep. And I can honestly say it's the most grown-up decision I've ever had to make. I don't think he got sick and died heroically, in the name of research for the book, but you have to admit, his timing was impeccable. Silly, gorgeous boy.

His kidneys had been on the wane for a few years and I knew, over the last few months, that he was going downhill rapidly. He'd lost a lot of weight, his appetite went on the blink, he drank water as if there was an impending drought only he knew about and his immune system was on overdrive, trying to cope with it all. Eventually, the vet couldn't feel one kidney at all, while the other was so large, and Dave was so thin even I could find it. And a knobbly thing it was too.

I had two choices – subject my 13-year-old boy to major exploratory surgery (probably only to confirm what we already suspected – the Big C) followed by.... what? Long, painful and prolonged treatment on a poor creature already severely weakened, with a slim chance it would do any good. Or to put him to sleep, quietly, calmly and in a dignified manner, on his favourite crinkly Waitrose carrier bag (only the best for my boy). The lovely vet, Grace, advised me to take him home, make him comfortable and let him eat whatever the hell he liked for a few weeks. A week later and I knew it was game over for him. I called and asked if the vet wouldn't mind coming to us; I didn't want to stress him out by levering him back into his basket for the one-way trip, and she agreed. Don't be shy to ask, it's not expensive; basically the cost of a double appointment – mine was less than £40 extra for a home visit – and vets are generally happy to come to you, for this type of thing.

I worked at home that morning, writing on my laptop with Dave beside me, snoozing on a cushion. Occasionally he'd take a piece of chicken from my hand, but no more than one. You could tell he was feeling nauseous: that salivary lip-licking and swallowing was getting worse. Then, about an hour before the vet came, he sat up and just looked at me for the longest time. We stared at each other and I thought, 'Yes, mate, it's time for you to exit stage left, and I think you just want this to stop now.'

So we did it at home. It was horrible, immensely sad, and lovely in equal measures. He just melted away as the vet nurse and I stroked him, and the vet did her thing. Then they took him away and he came back, a couple of weeks later, in a pretty box, all cremated and tidy.

He's currently sitting on a shelf, waiting patiently for me to get my fat backside into gear and get a plant in a pot for him to fertilise and for us to remember him by. RIP Dave the Rave, you are ever sorely missed.

I'm not sure why I'm writing this. Why I'm not trying to make you feel better about the inevitable loss of your beloved dog or imparting a morsel of comfort which may, or may not, help you. Probably it's because I can't make you feel better and nothing will help. For a while.

Maybe it's to say that it's all right to be the grown-up, it stinks but, as one friend put it 'I got divorced, then I lost my dog, who was my best friend. One recovers.' Ever the dry wit. She is right, though.

Whether you are looking for a sign to let you know it's the right time to let go, or it's a decision taken from you by the vet who's telling you it's the best thing, you will be able to do it, because it's part of the caring. It's part of the love.

Pets grieve too

For the next few days I couldn't bear to be near Nikita, I don't know if it's because I didn't want to feel the pain of losing her, too, or if I was too busy looking after Pearl, Dave's sister. I've never thought that Pearl felt anything much other than anxiety, and general sleepiness. For the most part he lived upstairs, she lived downstairs. But she had taken to sleeping right next to Dave those last few days, and now I couldn't get her off the crunchy carrier bag – not her style at all. I had to throw it away in the end, I couldn't bear to look at either the bag, or her sad expression.

It's not only you who feels the loss, you have other pets to comfort, to make feel safe. There was Pearl, pulling fur out of her backside for all she was worth, for weeks. It's calmed down now; time has soothed us both. Nikita didn't appear worried at all. I'll be a right old mess when she goes.

🐾 Allergies 🐾

After itchy queries, the most common conversation I have with first-time customers, by miles, is about allergies. Worried owners call to enquire about dog treats. They've had allergy testing done on their dog, either blood sampling or full-on skin testing under sedation, and it turns out 'that my dog is allergic to everything. Pork, beef, chicken... wheat, barley and maize... house, dust and storage mites ... grasses and pollens. You name it, my dog's allergic to it. Now what dog treats can he eat?' 'Err... sweet potato?' comes my weedy answer.

And I've always thought to myself: 'Surely it can't be right that all these dogs are allergic to all these things? There must be degrees of reactivity whereby a dog hasn't developed a true allergy but has reacted negatively to certain things? And every supposed allergy can't be an actual allergy; some must be an intolerance, or a sensitivity?' Turns out I'm right.

I asked the people who test for allergies for a living and here's what they told me: 'When your dog is having a reaction to something, however mild, understandably you want to know what triggers that reaction. Symptoms might be vomiting, itching and scratching, runny eyes and nose or smelly, itchy ears. The most common symptoms are classified into three groups: dermatalogical (the skin), gastrointestinal (the gut) and respiratory (the lungs, nose and throat). Symptoms begin when your body starts to think that something normal and everyday – a food or pollen, for example – is now dangerous. The reaction – the itching or vomiting – is your body's way of speaking up. It's the smoke signal sent up to let you know that there's trouble in paradise.'

It is estimated that 10-15% of the canine population in the UK will suffer from atopy (a reaction to many compounds that affects the skin) at one time or another. Many atopic reactions start in puppyhood with dogs growing out of them as they reach adulthood, just as we do. But, for the dogs who continue to react, the principal culprits will be changes in seasons, high pollen days, house dust mites and food – generally beef, wheat and cow's milk.

A true allergy is a disease that occurs when the immune system reacts abnormally to common, usually harmless, substances such as pollen, food or insects. It can also be genetic which means it will affect your dog for all his life and will need managing. However, mostly, while your dog may suffer an adverse reaction to something, *this is not a full-blown allergy*. If he suffers an adverse reaction to a food, for example, or builds up an intolerance over time, the resulting problem will generally be confined to the digestive system, whereas a full-blown allergy will trigger a strong immune response that could be life-threatening.

So how do you know if your dog has an allergy? Well, every dog has his own 'critical threshold', the point at which exposure to several allergens causes the level of stimulation to build up, pushing him over the edge, resulting in a flare-up.

To make matters more confusing, those thresholds vary from dog to dog, depending on his breeding, environment, vaccine history, diet... all sorts! You name it, it can have an effect on tolerance. So what sets one dog off chewing his back legs will be as nothing to another dog in the same house.

An allergy test should only be carried out after the obvious has been dealt with, i.e. a parasitic infection – fleas, mange, etc – or you've tried to determine if a certain food is the culprit. What you don't want to do is assume an allergy straight off, and end up making unnecessary and potentially stressful changes for the dog's entire life.

Food allergies and intolerances

If you think it could be a food allergy or intolerance then congratulations, you are today's winner! Because weeding out a food problem is going to be way easier than keeping the dogs away from grass and trees for ever, that's for sure. The way to sort this one out is with an elimination diet. You just have to be strong in the face of those big brown eyes and steel yourself against any begging, or emotional connection you have to food.

Try not to project it onto your dog, like the rest of us do. This is the time for fortitude and tough love.

The elimination diet

An elimination diet works like this. For 8-12 weeks feed your dog nothing but a protein and a carbohydrate source they haven't eaten before. Fish and rice, chicken and sweet potato, for instance. With a bit of luck, you'll be able to select the foods that are least likely to cause

Things that could be making your dog itch, scratch and vomit:	Inhaled allergens	Contact allergens
	Air fresheners	House dust and mites*
	Pollens – trees, grasses and seeds	Pollens – trees, grasses and seeds
Food allergens	Perfume	Fleas
Beef	Cigarette smoke	Flea control such as spot-on treatments
Pork	Mould spores	
Soy	Washing powder & fabric softener	Mould
Wheat		Flea, tick and mouse bites or faeces
Rice	Household cleaning products	
Maize (corn)		Dander (shed skin cells)
Sugars	Carpet & furniture fresheners	Feathers
Colours		Fabrics

*House dust mites are by far the biggest problem when it comes to allergies in the UK.

a problem. Just the diet plus water. No treats, no tidbits, no sneaking her a bit of food under the table at mealtimes. That's it. Simple, and yet really hard all at once. It's simple because you know where you are and what you're feeding her. It's hard because you have to get everyone in the house on board, keep all other food away from a pleading dog, and be able to resist that wistful stare.

The simple fact of the matter is, if you don't keep up with the elimination diet it's impossible to tell if it's a food allergy at all or if it's the 'snacks' causing the symptoms to continue. So be strong, be the grown-up, and reward yourself with a large glass of something on the first day that you're not confronted with

a large pile of sloppy, stinky, blood-infused poo. Rejoice in a firm stool, people! Rejoice!

I've done that, now what?

If feeding this simple ration has cleared up the symptoms it's pretty safe to say that food is what's causing your dog's issues. At the very least it's certainly not helping when it comes to tipping her over the edge and into crisis. So! This is good news all round. Make me a large G&T!

Now you've established that your dog's symptoms go away when she's only fed two foods and water, the next step is to start introducing new foods, one at a time. If you've been giving

'I don't
DO dairy!'

chicken and rice, try lamb and rice, see if it kicks off. If it doesn't, introduce fish and rice, then try fish and sweet potato, but just one thing at a time – otherwise, if the symptoms reappear, you won't know which food is stirring up trouble. If you get a reaction to a food, kick it into touch and don't feed it again. Ever. Over time, you'll narrow it down to a range of foods that don't trigger a reaction and can be safely fed to your dog.

Golden rule!

And if you're going back to feeding shop-bought dog food, never, ever, go back to one that lists the ingredients by category. If the label reads 'meat and animal derivatives' you won't know what's in it and the symptoms are very likely to reappear. Same goes for treats. Always read the label and choose food ingredients listed by the ingredient, i.e. chicken.

Allergy testing

If an elimination diet has got you nowhere useful, it could well be time for an allergy test. Allergy testing is done in one of two ways: serological allergy testing – i.e. a blood test; and intradermal testing – a skin test. Blood tests are carried out first, as skin-testing requires your dog to be sedated. Blood tests are comparable to skin tests and can be used for food allergens too, which skin tests are not great at detecting. In both tests, your vet is looking for potential allergens and antibodies that could be responsible for the adverse reaction in your dog.

Allergens contain protein, and almost anything can be an allergen. The most common are house dust mites, pollens and food, animal dander and insects.

In the presence of an allergen the immune system produces antibodies known as immunoglobulins. The allergy test looks for the proteins that make up these immunoglobulins. For example, in the case of digestive problems, an allergy test might look for an intolerance to lactose, food additives or histamine-releasing foods.

Here comes the science – how it's done

Blood serum taken from your dog is diluted and introduced to a panel of allergens on a micro-titre plate (looks a bit like a Connect 4 game, only smaller and horizontal).

There are three specific panels to choose from:

Food – meats, cereals, eggs, milk
Environmental – grass, trees, weeds, pollens
Secondary infection – malassezia and sarcoptic mange

The test reproduces what happens when an adverse reaction occurs in your dog, and then measures the antigens and antibodies produced in the sample. They're produced in such large numbers that a simpler way to grade a response is to group them together and number them from 1 to 5, 1 being the weakest response, 5 being the strongest.

And then the confusing bit...
So you have your allergy testing back from the vet and you've got a reaction of 2 for chicken, 3 for potato and 5 for beef. Then a 4 for meadow grass and a 3 for nettle. But it doesn't translate that your dog is allergic to all these things. Your dog may have scored a 2 on chicken and that low number will be enough to have him pulling his fur out, but his score of 4 on meadow grass triggers absolutely no reaction whatsoever. All the test means is antibodies have been detected. Your dog has had an immune response to something he used to see as normal but now views as the enemy.

To make matters even more confusing, these results can be skewed by many factors. If your dog has been vaccinated recently, has moved to an entirely new environment – say, from the coast to the countryside – or if a stranger moved into the house, human or animal, it matters not, the stress effect can be the same; and it can skew the results. All I can tell you is that allergy testing is your starting point. It doesn't have all the answers.

Buy One Get One Free

Not only that, but your dog may have more than one allergy, and it could be that the combination is what's pushing her over their threshold. If she only had the one allergy she may well have been OK, but two sets off her immune response, which is paw chewing for England.

Immunotherapy injections

If, through allergy testing, luck and a following wind, you and your vet have managed to pin down one or more specific non-food allergens that are triggering your dog's reactions (pollen, timothy grass or house dust mites, for instance) then a course of immunotherapy injections could well reduce symptoms to a minimum. It's unlikely that immunotherapy will cure your dog's allergy but you can get it to a stage where you will only get the odd, manageable flare-up.

In a simple analogy, immunotherapy

works like this: my mate Jerry is allergic to pet hair and yet he has a cat. I can pick up his cat, bury my face in her fur, inhale her lovely kitty smell and I only come away with a rude stare. It would put Jerry's immune system into a flat spin. He'd be on oxygen in the back of an ambulance nee-nah-nee-nah-ing his way to A&E in minutes. That's because pet hair triggers his immune response – his airways go on strike. So why does he have a cat, the silly sod? Well, Jerry's still alive and Dusty has reached the ripe old age of 19. Too old to run away from me and my fur-inhaling ways, much as she would like to.

Jerry knew he was allergic to cats but decided to get one anyway, figuring that with constant exposure to the dander and fur, his lungs would get over it. After a while his immune response calmed down. It only works with his own cat, though – and at arm's length! At my house you can always tell where Jerry is, just by following the sounds of coughing and snottiness as Pearl's fur finds its way up his nose.

By the same token, immunotherapy injections introduce tiny amounts of an allergen into your dog's immune system. If, for example, your dog reacts to timothy grass, over the course of injections his itching and scratching will lessen and flare-ups will be moderate and occasional rather than severe.

The vet will get the vial made up to your dog's specific requirements and keep it in the fridge for you to come in and get the dog injected, or you can probably do it yourself at home. If you're happy to try this, then the vet will show you how it's done. A lot cheaper for you and less stressful for the dog.

🐾 Food supplements 🐾

This is a fast-growing market both in the US and the UK. Just like the human supplement industry, quality varies massively, so you need to make sure you get the best quality for your money. To be honest, as long as your dog is getting everything he needs from his diet, he shouldn't generally need supplements. There are a few situations, however, in which specific supplements can make a real difference.

When I got Nikita, my little Bulgarian street dog, she was run-down, skinny and traumatised. She didn't have much fur, and her pink and black spotted skin looked a bit like a piglet's. After being rescued she'd been spayed and treated for mange but she still had a fungal skin problem. To top it all off, she had to get her rabies vaccination, in order to leave the country and travel. Rabies vaccinations don't make anyone feel great. So I got her straight on the echinacea for a couple of weeks. Echinacea is a herb plant from the daisy family with antibiotic and wound-healing properties. We humans use it to help stave off winter colds. I added it to her food to help build her

ANN & OLE

When Ole the gundog was a few months old he started to get very itchy ears and his eyes were runny and inflamed. Steroids were not helping because they only provided relief from scratching for a couple of weeks. Once the effect wore off, the itching cranked up again. Blood tests at 12 months revealed he was allergic to two particular grasses, and dairy products. He is now three and has been receiving immunotherapy injections for two years. Ann has seen a big improvement. 'We get occasional flare-ups. But Ole has had steroids only twice in the past two years – once for a sore eye, and once because he swiped someone's ice cream and got a sore ear! We manage on the occasional antihistamine and keep him off dairy. I also have him on salmon oil, Billy No Mates and Verm-X, so I'm avoiding spot-on flea and worm treatments too.'

DEB & WOODY

Woody was around eight months old when he started to lose all the fur around his eyes. The vet crossed mange off the list and did an allergy test. Turned out that poor Woody was allergic to four grasses and house dust mites, the most common allergen by far. The vet recommended a course of immunotherapy injections, every week for a month then every month for life.

Well, Woody didn't have a lot of fur left on his face and itched constantly so Deb went ahead with it. She kept the vial in the fridge and injected Woody herself. She also started to explore the benefits of a raw diet. After six months of injections and feeding Woody raw food his fur had grown back, he'd stopped rubbing his face along the floor to get relief and Deb no longer had to rub him down after a walk. Woody's now six years old, off the injections entirely, and Deb says they've had one bad summer since.

immune system back up. I also added plant and fish oils to the mix to encourage her fur to grow back, coupled with a good, low-grain food to discourage the fungus. In a few short months, she went from timid, smelly, bald thing to frisky, bouncy and lovely pain in the bum.

How do you choose a good supplement?

In the UK, medicines and remedies for pets are subject to regulation by the Veterinary Medicines Directorate (VMD), a branch of DEFRA. In order to make a health claim about a product and put it on the market, a company must first prove it to be effective, through research, product development and testing. However, supplements added to food are not regulated. For example, a natural 'remedy' for fleas has to be licensed but a food supplement to do the same job doesn't.

This is why most of the products you buy over the counter come as food supplements. It's a way for small companies to bring products to market without having to commit to the prohibitive expense of testing, which would put many of them out of business. However, this lack of regulation is a double-edged sword. On the one hand, you can try the natural route before you take a trip to the vet – for treating a flea allergy, for instance. On the other hand, you don't know if what you're buying is any good or just a tablet made of chalk and not much else.

What constitutes a good supplement?

In the end it comes down to these pointers:

Brand
Reputation
Word of mouth
Cost
Communication

These pointers may sound a bit nebulous, but they count for a lot. In fact, they're all you've got!

What you want, of course, is a product that does what it says it will. But research and quality ingredients cost money, and it's not always easy to tell if there's enough of the active ingredient in a product for it to be of any use in the first place. With supplements you generally do get what you pay for. Again, make sure you read the ingredients label and avoid the hype on the front of the box.

Talk to your pet shop, find out what customers are coming back for again and again, ask questions on forums and speak to the people who make them. As you read through this section of the book you'll start to get an idea of what to look out for.

Don't buy pet supplements from a supermarket. They will not be great quality. And buy supplements made for pets, not humans. Our needs are different from a dog's, which are different from a cat's, and so on. Don't skimp on quality because you won't get the benefit and it will be money down the drain.

Caveat emptor – buyer beware, and all that.

Supplements for the sick

If your dog has been on long-term steroids or antibiotics, or is receiving treatment you would like to stop, then natural is definitely worth exploring.

Supplements can also be taken alongside conventional, ongoing treatment to help mitigate the effects the medication is having on your dog. You can feed a probiotic while giving antibiotics to offset the effect on the gut. You can give echinacea on a short-term basis to help a dog on long-term meds to keep her immune system up and fighting.

The market for supplements that target specific problems is growing rapidly too – stiff joints, poor digestion, fur loss, itchy skin and bad (dog) breath are all well catered for.

Nikita had heinous dog breath and really slimy saliva (I know, it's truly gross). After six months on a tiny scoop a day of CSJ Seaweed and Parsley supplement I don't have to resist the urge to wretch if I get a passing lick on the face when I'm sitting on the floor. She's no longer slimy nor smelly, in the oral department, at least.

Before you go down the holistic route you need to make sure that your dog is healthy in the first place so you're not doing her more harm than good by giving her a product that exacerbates an undetected health condition. Firstly, and always, take your dog to the vet. If I get a call from a dog owner looking for something other than flea and worming treatment, it's the first thing I tell them to do if they haven't already.

The importance of understanding what you give your pet

You may want to give your dog a seaweed supplement to help keep her teeth clean, but if she suffers from hyperthyroidism you probably shouldn't because the iodine content in the seaweed could do more harm than good.

Did you know that St John's wort can increase your chances of bleeding during surgery and valerian can result in you needing more anaesthetic? Me neither, until I had an op last year. The questionnaire you fill in about your current medications includes a section on herbal medicine. It's because they do affect you, they do work, which is why they need to complement each other, not add to the burden on an already stressed body.

There's nothing wrong with getting a second opinion either. Try consulting a holistic vet. I'd contact Richard Allport in Potters Bar www.naturalmedicinecentre.co.uk. But there is bound to be someone near you and other dog owners local to you will have recommendations, for sure.

Herbs, oils and tablets

We tend to think supplements come as tablets in white plastic tubs. We take them for a week or so, then leave them, untouched and unloved, on top of the microwave for two years before we throw them out. Or that could just be me. But edible supplements come as herbs, tinctures and oils. Here's a little about each and why they work as they do.

Herbs

I rate herbs highly for dog ailments. They take a couple of weeks to get into the system and working so it's not a quick fix, more a way-of-life choice. But once at full tilt, their effects will be farther reaching and longer lasting than many pharmaceutical products because they tackle the underlying problem rather than alleviate the symptom.

Many modern medicines are founded on herbs. Most are now synthesised copies, though there's nothing wrong with that. Herbs contain vital minerals and nutrients that will contribute to the overall health, and therefore a stronger immune system, in your dog, which in turn gives you a healthier animal able to fend off disease. So yes, I am a herb lover!

Herbs work systemically, throughout the body; they don't just purge the system. Take, for example, a herbal wormer and flea repellent. For a parasite, coming up against a pharmaceutical treatment is like you or me being at a party, having a great time, mixing and socialising with all the other worms then being rudely ejected for no apparent reason when Advocate and Milbemax

decide we've outstayed our welcome. If you prefer outdoor events, partying with the fleas down at the tail end, your night ends abruptly as you're overcome by the fumes of Advocate or Frontline.

With the herbal equivalents, Billy No Mates and Verm-X, you're not invited to the party at all. And frankly the dog who's on the herbal is no longer the cool host he once was. He smells funny and your friends who did manage to get in aren't looking so hot; in fact, they look a bit sick as they're ushered back onto the grass, discreetly and without fuss so as not to bother the host.

Plus: herbs do not create any resistance and the extra nutritional value means the added bonus of glossy coats and less windy ways.

Oils – fish, veg & plant

Oils are also favourite supplements of mine. Cold-pressed oils can help with skin and coat condition, moulting, seasonal allergies, that doggy smell (caused by an imbalance of omega 3 and 6 in the gut), inflammation, pain relief, kidney function and vision, to name a few.

The components of the oils which really matter are the essential fatty acids. These are found in fish, vegetables and plants such as salmon, herring, flax-seed, starflower and evening primrose. They include omega 3 (linolenic acid), omega 6 (linoleic acid) and arachidonic acid, and are often not present in sufficient quantities in our pets' diets (or in humans', for that matter) so we could do with adding them.

The easiest way of getting omega 3 and 6 into the diet in the correct ratios is by feeding a specific blend of oily, cold-water fish (salmon, mackerel and herring for instance) mixed with good plant oils (flaxseed, starflower and sunflower oils).

The best oil I've found for this is Yumega Plus. The quality of the oils is second to none and all the guess-work around how much of each oil you need is taken care of for you. Dog show people love it for what it does for their dogs' fur, which gleams as they sashay and mince about the show ring. The blend of fish and plant oils gives your dog relief from hayfever-like symptoms of runny nose and eyes, sneezing and wheezing and, probably more than anything, itching skin and all the subsequent scratching and discomfort.

With oils you really do get what you pay for. So while lots of dogs get cod liver oil or evening primrose oil supplements added to their dinner, both will only contain small amounts of the omega 3 they need and not much omega 6. Equally, a common assumption around feeding a dog canned fish in oil is that he will get all the essential fatty acids he needs from the oil and fish in the tin. Well, the short answer is, they won't. Tinned fish is cooked in the can at

TREATMENTS AND SUPPLEMENTS FOR EVERY DAY

Food supplements for fleas, ticks, mites, mange and worms are out there and they work incredibly well. They've been working that way for thousands of years. It's only in the last 80 years or so that pharmaceutical parasite control has even existed. Before that it was nothing, or herbs. And the herbs do work.

- Use neem for bites, wounds, scratches, fungal problems
- Itchy skin? A change of diet, then add an oil supplement
- Atopic allergies? Omega oils
- Smelly dog? Probiotics

over 200°F which destroys any essential fatty acids, and the oil added won't be of the best quality, certainly not cold-pressed. Tinned fish can certainly be a great source of protein, but a home for essential fatty acids it ain't.

Omega oils as an added ingredient in pet food and treats will also have been heated with the same result. So, although it's good if they are included in food and treats, as I've said previously in the diet section, if you see them listed on the label after vitamins and minerals they really are there purely for marketing purposes.

Look after your oils. Essential fatty acids are delicate things and need a little TLC themselves if we're to get the best out of them. Always buy cold-pressed oils and store them in the fridge once opened. Another arch enemy of the essential fatty acid is oxygen, which starts to degrade the oil once the bottle has been opened. So only buy what you will use in three months or less to retain maximum effect. No one likes a rancid oil and it can be toxic. It can put you right off your breakfast, and might even revisit you shortly after consumption.

MY DOG IS VEGETARIAN. HOW DO I GET OMEGA OILS INTO HER?

Well, for starters, and I don't apologise for what I am about to say, your dog is not a vegetarian. She has teeth like that for a reason, and it's not for ripping into a carrot. Unless your dog has the rarest of food allergies to everything but vegetarian food, it's been your choice to go down that road. If you feed your dog a vegetarian diet then shame on you – a dog is an obligate carnivore and needs meat and fish. Now I've got that off my chest, there *is* a way of getting your Omega 3 from a vegetable source – although the highest levels by far are found in oily fish. Add flaxseed, rapeseed, soya oils and eggs fortified with Omega 3 to her diet. They're the best plant-based and dairy sources.

Virgin coconut oil

Virgin, or unrefined, coconut oil has a wide variety of benefits. It's known to aid the healing processes of many ailments, can help prevent yeast infections and has been found to reduce the risk of cancer. It's really good for skin conditions too. Rub it into rashes or small wounds to aid healing. Dogs generally love the taste of it. Buy a good-quality virgin oil and add it to her food at 1ml per 10 kilos of body weight per day.

Coconut oil is 90% saturated fat made up of shorter-chain fatty acids. Unlike other saturated fat, it doesn't have a negative effect on cholesterol. It contains lauric acid, which is also found in mother's milk and helps to build the immune system. It's also been found to contain antifungal and antibacterial properties.

YOUR SHOE BOX OF GOODIES

Here's a list of what you need and what it's for. I've arranged it in two categories, Ongoing, for continuous care, and As & when, for occasional use, so you don't need to dash out and buy everything all at once.

I've added these brands because I know they work very, very well, not because I sell them. Indeed, not all are on my website.

As I hope will have become evident by now, you don't need to keep an arsenal of natural weapons in your cupboard to keep your dog healthy; a small box will do.

ONGOING:

Product	What it's good for
Billy No Mates CSJ	Fleas, ticks, mites and mange
Verm X	Worms
Neem spray	Insect repellent Treating insect bites
Dorwest Roast Dinner toothpaste	Tooth-cleaning and fine doggie dining combined
Yumega Plus, and a drop of virgin coconut oil	Reduces moulting Reduces symptoms of allergies

AS & WHEN

Problem	Solution
Crud and bacteria deep in ears on big dogs	Bamboo cotton ear buds
Stiff joints and poor mobility	Yumove joint supplement
Poor gut health Restoring the gut after illness and medication Yeast overgrowth on skin and in ears	Yumpro
Ear mites and minor infections	Thornit powder
Minor eye irritations such as pollen dust Tear stains	Colloidal silver eye spray
Ear cleaning and maintenance	Colloidal silver ear drops
Bites, wounds and scratches Minor infections Insect repellent	Ekoneem
Itchy skin and scratching Fungal skin problems Clearing parasites and eggs away Insect repellent	Neem shampoo
Tick removal	O'Tom Tick Twister or fine-pointed tweezers

Mindfulness
for dogs

Let your dog be a dog

⋯⋯⋯⋯⋯⋯⋯⋯ 🦴 ⋯⋯⋯⋯⋯⋯⋯⋯

Some useful advice on training and behaviour

A dog's mental well-being is just as vital to her long-term health as fulfilling her physical needs. Knowing what's going on inside your dog's head, understanding what she requires in terms of physical contact, interaction with others, emotional support and mental stimulation, then giving it to her, will keep your dog healthier and happier for longer.

I would like to quote at this point from a very interesting book, *Mental Health and Well-being in Animals*, written by Franklin D McMillan and published in 2005. McMillan says: 'No distinct line separates the human mind from the non-human mind. The more science learns about the animal mind, the more difficult it is to believe that the mental lives of non-human animals are fundamentally different from ours, that they somehow feel pain differently, feel less pain, feel physical pain but not emotional pain, or don't feel pain or suffer emotional distress at all.'

It is only our arrogant human mind that makes a distinction between *them* – all the other animals in the world, and *us* – the superior humans. So, while it's widely accepted that animals are sentient creatures, we think of them, albeit subconsciously, as being somehow less

than us when it comes to their mentality.

As pet owners we know that dogs feel emotion, they have perception, they have an opinion, and it's a subjective one. A dog, like her human, has a point of view. We don't need to see a peer-reviewed paper to convince us. And yet, while we treat our pets with respect – love them, feed them the best food we can find, spare no expense on vet visits and medication – we often neglect the emotional and mental needs which make the lives of our dogs so much more than the sum of their parts.

Take leaving the house, for instance. If you leave a dog home alone all day, five days a week, then come home and do what you do at night – hobbies, watching TV, a long soak in the bath – and don't do anything much with your dog, she is going to be sad, lonely and depressed. She just is. As you would be if your carer just scratched you under the chin once in a while. If you don't like to let your dog off lead on a walk, because you're worried she won't come back to you, she won't be getting any pleasure out of life on that front either. Dogs need to seek out, pause and sniff; it stimulates their brains massively. They need to be free to run. This is a normal dog displaying normal dog behaviour. It's vital that if you're getting a dog you factor in the time and effort needed to keep him or her in good shape mentally and emotionally.

WHICH BRINGS ME BACK TO PARTS 3 AND 4 OF THE ANIMAL WELFARE ACT WHICH STATES THAT PETS:

3. Need to be able to exhibit normal behaviour patterns
4. Need to be housed with, or apart from, other animals

As one fellow dog owner said to me recently, 'Still too many of us adore our dogs when it suits us, but are able to put them out of our minds when we need to, somehow imagining that they will close down operations until we reawaken them on our return. Not so! When my dog walker can't do her normal two-hour stint, or comes in well after lunch rather than by one o' clock, Pip is actually depressed. It's horrible. He is all quiet and withdrawn; and I feel I need to be carted off by the RSPCA.'

I know Pip is the most loved and cared for of dogs. I also know that the majority of us have to go out to work for a living, and we also think the same way, that our dogs will go into 'sleep' mode while we go about our business, until we return, when they can be hopeful of some attention.

New research, conducted by Attila Andics from the Comparative Ethology Research Group, placed 12 dogs, trained using positive reinforcement methods – i.e. 'If I lie still for a few minutes I'll get so much praise and lots of treats, I won't know what to do with myself' – in MRI scanners, fully awake, to see how they reacted to voices and sounds. Emotionally charged sounds, such as laughter and crying, set off similar responses in their brains as they do in our own. If the dog's owner left the scan room briefly then re-entered, the dog's emotional response could be clearly seen on the MRI. Attila Andics said, 'We think dogs and humans have a very similar mechanism to process emotional information.'

Gregory Berns is a professor of neuroeconomics at Emory University and the author of *How Dogs Love Us: A Neuroscientist and His Adopted Dog Decode the Canine Brain*. In an article he wrote for the *New York Times* in 2013, recounting his research with his dog Callie and other MRI canine volunteers, he stated that: 'The ability to experience positive emotions, like love and attachment, would mean that dogs have a level of sentience comparable to that of a human child. And this ability suggests a rethinking of how we treat dogs. If we went a step further and granted dogs rights of personhood, they would be afforded additional protection against exploitation. Puppy mills, laboratory dogs and dog racing would be banned for violating the basic right of self-determination of a person.

'I suspect that society is many years away from considering dogs as persons. However, recent rulings by the Supreme Court have included neuroscientific findings that open the door to such a possibility. In two cases, the court ruled that juvenile offenders could not be sentenced to life imprisonment without the possibility of parole. As part of the rulings, the court cited brain-imaging evidence that the human brain was not mature in adolescence. Although this case has nothing to do with dog sentience, the justices opened the door for neuroscience in the courtroom. Perhaps someday we may see a case arguing for a dog's rights based on brain-imaging findings.' Hence this section on training and behaviour.

Judgmental, much?

My good friend, Helen O'Donnell had her first baby three months after I got Nikita. She never thought she'd have a baby, wasn't even sure she wanted one. Then she met the lovely man that is Gary, got pregnant and fell headlong into a world of outrageous and blatant judgemental opinion – barely disguised as 'support and advice'. Helen has also had many dogs in her life so she wasn't particularly shocked by it. Because it's exactly the same for dog owners. Everyone has an opinion.

So there we were, Helen and the bump (now Chloe), me and Nikita, walking around the park one day, and we got to talking about how everyone's an expert when it comes to dogs and kids. I asked her, as an expectant, first-time mum, what were the main subjects she felt she was being scrutinised on. 'My choice of nappy, and breastfeeding,' came the snap answer. She didn't even have to think about it. For me it was what I was feeding Nikita and why I had her in a harness.

It's human nature to judge, Helen

For the definition of dog see 'toddler' in the dictionary

and I freely admit to being just as opinionated as everyone else and we're fine with being judged right back. Let's face it, we've got two chances, fat and none! We are all busybodies, sticky beaks, armchair experts and we want you to know precisely what we think of the way you're handling your dog and feeding your child.

So suck it up, buttercup. Just do your best and ignore the rest. Train your dog in the basics, teach him how to behave in public and in private, learn to understand what your dog needs and what his body language is really telling you and you'll be fine.

Also, and I know this is incomprehensible, realise that some folk just don't like dogs, in the same way others just don't like kids. Or sprouts. And that's okay, too. Teach your dog to sit and not jump up at new people, always scoop their poop and put it in the bin, and you won't be adding grist to their mill.

★ Behaviour ★

Before you start working with your dog, to get a better understanding of where he's coming from, it's good to stop for a moment and look at life from his perspective, where he is in the pecking order (just below the kids and just above your other half!), and to realise that he doesn't have a clue what you're talking about.

A dog is, in essence, a two-year-old toddler. I know we tend to anthropomorphise our dogs, give them human traits, but really a two-year-old is about their level. A dog has no idea of right and wrong, no impulse control and no conscious desire to be anything other than a survivor, which makes him the most adorable, loving and cuddly parasite you're ever likely to encounter.

We are the ones who will say: 'Ronnie's looking guilty, what's he done?' But Ronnie's not thinking that way; he just reads our body language, which is saying something has annoyed us.

'I have water
in my ears
so cannot
hear you.
Soz!'

He then goes into appeasement mode – licking his lips, making himself small. He's saying, 'Don't harm me, I'm no trouble'. He's learned that behaviour; he hasn't understood a word we've said; he's just picked up that something's not right with us.

The dominance theory doesn't hold water either. A dog wants to be a part of something; he has no interest in being in control or being pack leader; he just wants to belong to his group in order to remain safe and fed. A dog has no ego.

There's a really good cartoon, I forget who by, of a man and his dog having a one-way conversation. Under the heading 'what you say' is a picture of the man talking to his dog and in the speech bubble coming from the man's mouth are the words: 'Time for your walk. Do you want a treat?' Underneath is a repeat of the same image with the heading 'what your dog hears' – only this time the speech bubble reads: 'blah, blah, walk, blah, blah, treat, blah.' It's brilliant because it captures the one big truth that never ceases to surprise us – our pets don't speak human. They react to our body language, eye contact, hand signals and the tone of our voice. That's pretty much it. We can spout any old garbage – it's all the same to them.

Put yourself in your dog's position

So before we start, just for a moment, I really want you to do this exercise, so you can get an understanding of what it's like to be your new dog. Read this next bit then chill out, lie back, close your eyes and really go there.

Imagine you're going to South Korea to stay with a host family for a couple of weeks. (It could happen!) You get a message that your English-speaking guide has been waylaid and you're to make your own way to your host's home. No matter, you'll be fine. However, as soon as you clear customs and start looking for the sign telling you where to catch the bus into town, you realise that you are now, effectively, illiterate. All the signs, everywhere, are in Korean (thoughtless Koreans, using their own language and all). You jump on what you think is the right bus to the right part of town and, by some miracle, you find your way there. This is when things start to get really strange. Because everything looks familiar but it's all completely different and you don't know the rules.

You're welcomed by a lovely, friendly lady who speaks no English and shown to your room, where she leaves you to it. You take a shower, because you feel like death warmed up after a 14-hour flight and you don't want to smell like the fetid camel's armpit in front of your kind hosts. You're feeling a little shy, and you just want to sleep for a week, but don't want to appear rude, so you sidle into the living room to introduce yourself. Only you can't. Because you don't speak their language and they don't speak yours. So what're you going to do? How

over or get in the way, all the while feeling very welcome but somehow alien and a little bit disruptive to normal proceedings on a Tuesday evening in suburban Seoul. The minute you think it's polite to do so – not too early, not too late, but what do you know about anything? – you make your excuses and head off to bed, utterly relieved. You can stand down now, get some rest. And hope your English-speaking guide shows up in the morning.

Thankfully she does, and after a good night's sleep you no longer feel as if your eyes are a sandpit. You discuss the night before and what you got up to in her absence and she goes quiet. Not only did you not remove your shoes

are you going to get through dinner, smalltalk and make it to bedtime without offending anyone or embarrassing yourself?

Sign and body language. That's how. You will muddle your way through the evening, eating politely, smiling at your hosts and trying not to knock anything on entering the house but you didn't bring slippers with you either. To make matters worse, you left your chopsticks sticking out of the rice in your bowl, instead of leaving them on the chopstick rest. Rookie mistake! That's about as rude as it gets.

But how were you to know? You didn't have a guide to school you in the subtleties of Korean etiquette. You feel awful and are afraid you won't be welcome again.

And that's what it's like to be a new dog in a new home. Everyone looks familiar. But no one speaks your language, you don't know who anyone is, what the rules of the house are, who's in charge or what they're going on about. All you can do is be polite, try not to wee on the carpet and slope off to your new bed at your earliest convenience. Hopefully, after a good night's sleep, someone will turn up to show you the ropes.

How stressful it is for a dog, whose sole aim in life is to please you, when he doesn't have the first clue what's expected of him. It's just like teaching a small child. He comes with his own innate behaviours you cannot change, but he's like a sponge and will absorb new stuff you teach him. He just needs practice, patience and understanding.

From working hound to couch potato pooch

Originally, we bred dogs to work for us.

We all had to sing for our supper back then. Dogs are used to having to work to maintain a roof over their heads. They were bred to herd livestock, guard our crops and protect us, not to lie about on the sofa for hours at a time, which is what the majority of dogs do these days. Dogs have evolved to fit in with our routine and we lead busy, hardworking lives, which means the dog is often left to his own devices. The advantage for a dog is that he's warm, dry, fed, not in any imminent danger, and loved, so he's not going anywhere. But he is bored out of his tiny brain quite a lot of the time, and isolation and a lack of socialisation, especially with other dogs, leads to fear, depression and possibly to aggression.

What a dog needs

On any given day your dog needs to eat, drink, exercise, sleep (preferably near you and any other animals in the house) and socialise. He needs to occupy his brain by chewing, sniffing and scavenging. He also needs to be thinking... which is where training comes in.

He may well be able to cope with being alone for a few hours while you work, but not all day, and not if he also sleeps alone at night and not if he only gets walked at weekends. It just doesn't work like that. Dogs are not built that way.

It's no wonder some dogs are so quiet ('no trouble' doesn't mean your dog's happy necessarily, just that there's just nothing to get excited about), or so destructive, or that they pee in the house, or growl at the children (who are getting all the attention), is it?

I'm going on, I know, but I've learned more about my dog through putting myself in her position than by doing anything else. Nikita can get by on two walks a day but they need to be good ones. Now she's recovered from living on the streets, physically at least, I can see collie in her, in both looks and behaviour. She's bright, energetic, needs to know where everyone is at any given time and she loves to run and play with other dogs. Luckily for me, though, she hates wind and rain, so on days when it's lashing down she's more than happy to hop out for a series of quick pees throughout the day and stay in bed. Our lurcher, Bud, liked a good 40-minute dash about, and then he was on the sofa for the rest of the day, thank you very much. It's what lurchers and greyhounds love to do.

I work full-time, in a building that doesn't allow pets, so I have a dog walker four days a week and my lovely friends Deb and Ging do the daytimes for me on Wednesdays. It's a cost I had to factor in when I got Nikita; it's part of the cost of owning a dog. Think of it as a

replacement for that gym membership you don't use.

If I don't take her out she actually starts to chew the furniture. She's had a go at my office chair-legs (metal), the corner of the sofa (fabric) and a bench (wood). She is an equal opportunities chewer. She's bored, fidgety and needs to get her message across. 'Take me out to the park, or the dining table gets it!' Another reason to take care choosing a dog that fits in with your lifestyle.

Normal behaviours – *Game of Thrones*, anyone?

Different dogs display normal behaviours according to their breed. Remember they won't necessarily fit into your home environment well, no matter how cute or desirable they are. Which is why it's crucial you select the right breed of dog based on your life now, not out of nostalgia for your childhood collie or because *Game of Thrones* stars a cute Northern Inuit.

If the Northern Inuit was a human it would be Tom Hiddleston. Utterly beautiful to look at, lots of fun to have around and extremely intelligent. On the flip side he suffers from extreme separation anxiety (no good if you're out all day), can be very rambunctious and loves to dig up your garden (hopeless if you like growing lovely things) – I'm talking about the dog, of course, not Tom, though I'd pay good money to get him round to dig up my herbaceous borders. So to speak. The same can be said for huskies and Alaskan malamutes. Both should be out in sub-zero temperatures hauling sledges, not lying on the sofa in your centrally heated home, moulting quietly as they pine for you – for anyone – to come home.

Opinionated I may be, but it's true nonetheless. Choosing the right breed of dog for your lifestyle is the best way to eliminate a range of behaviours that, while normal for the dog, will cause considerable upset and possibly lead to you having to give up your much-loved pet. Note, for example, that the number of rehomed and abandoned huskies, Alaskan malamutes and Northern Inuits has soared since *Twilight* and *Games of Thrones* came into our lives. Just as other breeds in other TV shows did before them and will again.

So I buried my bone, so what?

Collies are made to herd, retrievers are bred to fetch things, while terriers like to dig a hole and bury stuff. We never think Ronnie, our Bedlington terrier, is grateful for a bone because he buries it instead of chewing it, whereas Nikita will decamp to the garden with hers to chew for hours, away from the beady gaze of the ever-watchful seagulls. And yet they're both probably just as happy with a bone because they get to display their breed behaviour. Digging works for Ronnie, while chewing hits the spot for Nikita. Another reason to bury food is to save it for a rainy day. If you're being fed too much, but you're predisposed to living the feast or famine life, you're going to hoard food, which is why you may find your dog in bed with a bone she's buried there. She's saving it for later.

Teach your dog to trade

Normal dog behaviours can be chewing, digging, barking at the doorbell or at strangers as they pass the house, and guarding. They guard that which they prize highly – their home, food, crate, your bed, you – which can be extremely irritating and noisy. Any dog will guard if it's not taught how to trade. A dog needs to learn that human hands bring things; they don't just take them away. A good way to get something off your dog if you don't want him to have it (your very expensive Love Alert Mac lipgloss) is to give him something else that's better, in dog terms. Remember, you're not rewarding bad behaviour – your dog doesn't get our meaning of good and bad – you're distracting him from the thing you want back, by giving him something he wants more, a treat or toy, for instance. After all, Love Alert really isn't his colour.

Learned behaviours

Your dog is engineered to go with his gut, to rely on his instincts to survive in the wild, so everything you teach him is a learned behaviour – sit, stay, leave, etc. The same goes for negative behaviours: if your dog was kicked or taunted by small children before she came to you, chances are she will be wary of small children. Your dog is also fairly well self-taught and is watching you for ways she can learn from you – the clever so-and-so. Nikita will whine when we're in the car as soon as we pull up at a place she regards highly – our house, my friend Deb's place (treats, walks and a comfy bed all happen there), the seafront or a country walk car park. She's saying, 'Don't leave me in the car, let me out!' She has learned that if she whines, she gets let out of the car – though I'm not sure where she's picked that up as the only time I leave her is to pop into a shop on the way home, when she just goes to sleep! At home she runs down

the hallway, past my coat, only pausing to give it a little nip. It means 'Take me with you.' She also watches me from the bedroom window, looming down on the car as I get in. I used to feel guilty and thought this was the ultimate in doggie emotional blackmail, but I quickly learned that she's waiting for me to leave the house so she can get to work on the cat food.

I'm not talking to you again, ever!

I used to shout this at my mum, whenever we had a fight. I'd go to my room vowing to never speak to her again. Until dinner time. At least! I thought this would make her suffer. She thought, 'Thank God for that, a bit of peace and quiet, you can stay there all night!'

Dogs appear to have moods, too. If I stick Nikita in the shower, to wash off her dirty paws and the odd muddy bit of fur, she's fairly tolerant and I'm soon forgiven. Subject her to the Full Monty, though, shampoo all over and a nail clipping, and I'm dead to her for the rest of the day, and all that night. She sleeps downstairs, depriving me of her dog breath, rabbit kicks and whiny dreaming. I get a good night's sleep; she thinks I'm upstairs, suffering. We're all happy.

When is bad behaviour not bad behaviour?

When it's pain or suffering. Because you're living with Koreans and you'll only ever get to grips with the basics of the language, it's nigh on impossible to let your hosts know that you've got an awful toothache, your hips are giving you grief or you're just not having a good day, and your bounce has boinged off somewhere else. You're sure it will be back soon, but you'd like a duvet day, time to lick your front legs relentlessly, because you've chipped a tooth and licking helps with the pain.

It's important to remember that to show pain is to admit to weakness, and you don't do that in the wild. It's better to get aggressive and get everyone to back off because they think you're a badass, than to hang about, whimpering because you've got a thorn lodged in one of your paw pads.

If your dog is a bit snappy, is growling at you and doesn't want to leave the house, and it's out of character for her to behave this way, it might be that she's just not

Only that's not what's happening at all. It's worry. She's just had to endure a bath she can't stand and a nail clipping that makes her very nervous so she's keeping her distance, staying away from the supposed danger until she's over it. That, and she's wary in case I subject her to any other intolerable and horrifying acts of love and care.

well. It's always good to check your dog over for signs and symptoms of illness, and if it persists get them checked out at the vet's.

We're pretty instinctive creatures, and not bad at knowing when our dog is happy, moody, unwell or scared without really consciously thinking about it. But if a dog bites someone it's because he's run out of options. A dog will do anything not to fight, because he's likely to risk injury to himself if his victim fights back. Growling is usually quite far down the line too. Before he gets to growling, or worse, he's given you plenty of signs he's not a happy bunny, and you need to learn what those signs mean and remove him from the situation that's making him fear for her own safety.

Sometimes Nikita will growl instantly or start barking for no apparent reason. Usually it's when we're in the house, so she's defending us, or when she's out on a lead and she needs to warn a dog she doesn't like (beagles and huskies – go figure) to stay away. She can hear things way before I pick up on them. But I'm never going to train that out of her, because I don't want to. It's not an escalating problem and it's not that common. If she barked every time the doorbell went or when anyone walked past the house, I'd train her using positive methods. Then, when someone walked past the house it'd be associated with a good thing – i.e. I don't bark, I get a treat.

What you don't want is the dog at DEFCON 1. The Defence Readiness Condition is an alert system used by the US military to determine the current state of readiness at any given time. States of readiness range from DEFCON 5 – everything is rosy – to DEFCON 1 – all-out war. Your dog has states of readiness, her own early-warning system. Biting is DEFCON 1 – you neither want nor need to go there. Learn the early-warning signs and remove your dog from the situation she's reacting to.

If you scold your dog when she tries to run away from something she's scared of, or growls at someone, you've taken that layer of safety away. In the end she's only got one option left, DEFCON 1!

Socialise, socialise, socialise

A lack of socialisation is the leading cause of fear and aggression in dogs. They don't need to have been mistreated to display negative behaviour; often they just haven't been well socialised.

Well-known dog behaviourist Gwen Bailey states that there is a special period, from birth up to around 12-16 weeks, during which puppies will accept new things they're exposed to. During that period, puppies need to have lots of pleasant encounters, with people, children, other animals and the outside world in general (from the moment they're allowed out). After that, the window closes, unfamiliar people and objects will be approached with caution and the dog may become wary and fearful. So exposure to pleasant and positive experiences very early on is key to raising a relaxed and happy dog.

When a dog is fearful of everyday things – children in school uniform (Nikita), other dogs (BB), men in hats (Bud) – it's often because they haven't been socialised early on as puppies or because they've had negative experiences at the hands of that particular group.

If you've never been socialised, if you've been kept in a cage or not walked, then suddenly you're out in the big, wide, noisy and confusing world, you're going to wet yourself right there and then, no doubt about it. Imagine, you're two feet tall, you've never seen anything but the back garden and the block around your house. Suddenly, you're in a car and on your way to town. Once there, it's all legs milling about, pointy shoes missing you by inches, and the sounds are atrocious: people shouting into mobile phones, trucks roaring past, motorbikes and cars. Then, you're having lunch (well, she is; no sausages appear to be forthcoming but then you're too scared to eat) and people are bending down to stroke you.

You can't see where their hands are because they're going over the top of your head, their faces are looming down at you, smiling (baring their teeth) and you're transfixed by the really hairy nostrils on the old guy who's trying to scratch your ears. You're dying inside. Your fight or flight response is dialled right up to max and you're doing all you can to back yourself in between the chair and the wall, or to run out the door and down the road. Anything to make it stop!

If I was that dog I'd have a hard job keeping a lid on it. Wouldn't you? Blimey, if I've got one of my bad headaches and someone won't leave me alone then they're going to know, in no uncertain terms, that they need to shut up. I'll ask politely a couple of times but after that, no more Mrs Nice Guy. Dogs are no different.

A dog will become aggressive in order to defend herself from something she fears but she's given you plenty of warning signs she's scared before she snaps. For a brilliant illustration of the most common body language postures and what they mean, go to Lily Chin www.doggydrawings.net.

Dogs and children

I am fortunate enough to have a few tiny humans in my life, including my goddaughter, Iris, who's terrified of dogs. I also have a dog who's afraid of small children. Introducing them to each other has been my hardest dilemma since I got Nikita. It's human nature to want everyone to get on. I like you, and I like you, so why don't the two of you like each other? Well, they have a mutual fear which makes perfect sense to both of them.

Iris is three and to her dogs are big, quick and unpredictable creatures. Nikita is a middle-aged lady, in dog terms, and she's definitely had run-ins with smallish children, especially school kids, judging by the way she reacts to a uniform. So what am I and Iris's mum to do?

I have to help Nikita overcome her fear of small people, and between us Sophie and I have to teach Iris, and her sister Edie, how dogs behave and how to act safely around Nikita. They'll be fine; we just need to take our time, not force anything and make the whole thing a positive experience for everyone involved.

Take it slowly

Like I say, the way to introduce them is to educate the children who are old enough to understand these things: take it slowly, don't force either party and make it a positive experience for everyone. You may have a dog who's been around kids before, but who hasn't been around these kids so she has to learn their particular behaviours, and as we know, small people, and dogs can become easily overwhelmed. Make sure you have lots of treats to hand, and not just for the dog!

What children need to know about dogs

1. Respect the dog

2. A dog is not a toy

3. Don't approach a dog you don't know

4. Always ask the grown-up if it's OK to stroke the dog before you approach it

5. No tugging or pulling at the dog's ears or tail

6. Only give the dog a treat or any food if you ask the owner first.

7. No shouting and squealing around the dog, it will become frightened

8. Don't drop food from the table for the dog to eat – some human food is poisonous to dogs.

9. The dog's stuff is off limits – toys, food, treats, water, bed or crate. If you're the sort of kid who likes to make camps in the house, don't ever do it in the dog's crate

10. Don't approach the dog at mealtimes or when she's sleeping. How would you react if someone came and shook you awake or shouted in your ear?

11. Treat the dog as you yourself would like to be treated

12. Don't tease the dog, especially with food

13. Don't try to dance with the dog or pick her up – you'll scare her or even injure her All four paws should be on the floor

14. Sudden movements can frighten a dog

15. Dogs say hello by sniffing, it's OK if she sniffs your leg, your hand or your schoolbag

Introducing dogs and children who are scared of each other

1. Arrange to meet in an open space – a park, for instance, or the beach, somewhere it's relatively quiet, like an outdoor café in the park

2. Let them see each other but keep some distance and approach each other naturally, as you would if you were meeting a friend in the street

3. Ask the kids not to stare at the dog, as dogs see this as a threat

4. Keep the dog on a long lead so it can get away but you still have control

5. Get the children to sit down, give them something to do, and let the dog approach in her own time

6. If you're introducing a dog from one household to children from another it's good to wait until you have sit and stay commands and not jumping up sorted out.

7. Teach the children that a dog says hello by sniffing so they don't jump when she approaches them, or they feel those tickling whiskers and a cold wet nose on their legs

8. Ask the kids to keep their voices calm, no high-pitched screaming especially, and to speak at a normal level

9. If the dog is calm and happy get her to sit with the children

10. If the children want to offer the dog treats, ask them to drop them on the floor initially for her to pick up

introduce a child. If the dog feels she can't get away and is terrified she's liable to snap

NB. Throughout this introduction, and always, for that matter, let your dog walk away when she's had enough.

Children and dogs can be lifelong friends, for the life of the dog at least. Looking after a dog can teach a child respect for others and build confidence. That said, you should always play it safe. A child has to be 10 years old to be legally allowed to look after a dog alone and I would never leave young children and dogs in a room, unattended. If I'm busy and there are small kids and dogs in the house, I split them up. The dog can go in the garden with a bone while the kids are inside getting busy with the crayons, or X-box – whatever works for you.

If your child isn't old enough to be responsible for walking the dog, then helping prepare meals, fetching leads and teaching the dog tricks are great ways to create a bond and help her feel that the dog is part of the family and not a threat to her.

11. If the dog is happy to be stroked, get the kids to stroke under her chin or along her back, not on her head. It's a normal thing to want to do but she will see it as a threat as the hand passes over her face and out of sight, and she will become scared.

12. After you've had the introduction let the dog go do her thing for a while, sniffing the grass, chasing another dog, whatever she likes, to de-stress.

13. Play with the kids and then try to introduce a game you can all play together – throwing a Kong stick* for the dog, teaching her a trick together – all rewarded with lots of treats

14. Teach the kids that dogs are not toys, they must be treated with respect

15. Don't hold your dog while you

*I'd recommend using a rubber stick like a Kong SafeStix. Vets see many stick injuries each year where the dog has run to catch a stick, only for it to pierce the roof of her mouth or get lodged in her throat, causing terrible injuries.

A dog wants to be part of something - it wants to belong...

Training

Fenton! Fenton! Fennnntoonnnnnn!

If you haven't seen the YouTube video I'm referring to, just type in Fenton + Richmond Park. It's been watched millions of times now and shows a poor bloke chasing his dog, Fenton the Labrador. Fenton, in turn, is chasing the deer that live and roam freely in the park. The deer have taken off in terror at a rate of knots, causing a near pile-up on the main road. There's no way that dog is coming back and, to be fair to Fenton's owner, Fenton's chase instinct means he won't hear a word of it, and he probably should have been on a lead, but who hasn't been caught out? I know I have. Luckily, not with anything like the same catastrophic results and no one was filming it on their phone!

On a different note, but a far more common one, I often meet dogs in my local park or on the beach who try to play chase with Nikita but they're not allowed off the lead. The owners tell me that the dogs won't come back so they're never allowed to run freely. It's flippin' tragic, and sad for the owner; but not half as tragic as it is for the poor dogs who never get the run they so desperately need and want.

This is yet another area where researching the breed you want will really count towards a happy life for everyone. Some dogs were bred for hunting, others for herding, so training that impulse out of your dog will take longer. If you want a collie, for example, you won't want one bred from working stock; get a puppy from a reputable breeder, who *isn't* bred for working. Then it's just a case of putting the practice in.

Essentially, we all get the dog we deserve. The more time and effort we put into training, the happier and more relaxed we'll all be.

Manners maketh the mutt

Although I may be in my late forties, if I forget to say please or thank you I hear my mum tut-tutting in my head at my poor manners. I was taught how to behave, how to conduct myself and what was and was not acceptable behaviour by my parents.

> Time + patience + effort + love = a well-rounded dog you can take anywhere and leave with anyone

My dad was a Coldstream Guard – bearskin, gleaming boots, the whole nine yards. I was a well-behaved child.

Your furry toddler needs training, but in reverse to the way you might think. Let me put it this way: if your dog jumps up at visitors when they enter your home, you think that by training your dog to sit when they enter, you've trained him not to jump up. But you haven't. You've trained him in another behaviour, one that you deem acceptable. You've trained him to sit. He can still jump up, but he's learned that he gets a better reward – a treat, or a toy, or a more favourable reception – when he sits.

We don't de-train a dog not to jump up. We train our dogs to do the things we _do_ want them to do.

The following are basic things you need to work on with your dog:

Focus
Getting your dog's attention and making eye contact, then holding it. Start by holding it for one second, then build up.

Physical contact
Get your dog used to being touched, held and stroked all over. She's going to be handled a lot of the time – by the vet, the groomer, the children and by you. Help her see it as a positive experience.

How to get on with people
Teach her how to greet people politely, how to greet children, and how to get on with other animald she meets.

Environment
Get her used to encountering everyday things – traffic, different homes, floor surfaces, noises.

Basic obedience
There are seven basic obedience techniques you and your dog need to master. After all, you're a team now so you're on a learning curve too.

Sit
Stay – wait
Down
Leave
Recall – coming back when called – in different places
Walking nicely on lead
Impulse control – jumping up, chasing etc

There's no need to get stressed about training your dog. You can make it very easy on yourself by enrolling both of you on a dog training and obedience course to get the fundamentals under your belt, then it's just a case of practising. Again, ask your vet, or dog-owning mates for a recommendation. If, like Nikita, your dog completely closes down in a room full of other dogs, invest in a little one-to-one training. A few lessons will change your life together for the better, I can guarantee it.

Practice makes perfect. 'Paw. Other paw'

It's sad, I know, but I'm proud of Nikita when she masters something I'm teaching her. I was chuffed to bits when she caught on to 'sit, paw, other paw' in return for treats. My goal is to teach her to roll over and play dead, which will be quite easy for her; she just needs the right motivation (treats) and for me to break the trick down for her into easy stages.

It says more about my idle ways that she can't do it already than her ability to learn. I find teaching tricks a bit, well, tricky half the time. And yet there's really nothing to it. There are plenty of videos on the internet that will show you a breakdown of a trick. The good news is that you only practise it for three minutes at a time so they don't get bored. It takes longer to boil the kettle and make tea than it does to teach a dog a trick.

If you want to wear those Jimmy Choos again, train your dog

If you always do what you've always done, you'll always get what you've always got. If your dog likes to chew your shoes/furniture/very expensive make-up (delete as appropriate), he will only stop it if you give him something better to do – reward him for doing something else, rather than punish him for chewing your stuff. Punishing him will only stress him out, and a great way for a dog to de-stress is to chew!

You can apply this logic to every unwanted behaviour in your dog. As well as training our dogs to do what we want them to do, as much as possible, we have to find ingenious ways to prevent them from doing the things we can do nothing about. As a for instance, I can't stop Nikita stealing the cat's food the minute I leave the house. I just can't. She was starving before I got her so she'll take it any way she can get it and it's never going to change. I can go out to the car to get something, come back in less than a minute and she's at it. We're currently learning the 'leave' command but I think her instinct is so strong that when I leave the house 'leave' won't figure one iota. So I've added a cat flap to the kitchen door and I close the door when I go out. That way the cat gets to eat and Nikita doesn't get fat. It's a win-win compromise and no one gets stressed.

For the first few months I had Nikita, she wouldn't ask to go out for a pee because she's timid, so would find a nice rug and do it on that, rather than draw attention to herself. For months! Seriously, I've had that rug out on the patio and given it a monumental scrub down – it's too good to throw out and it's a nice thing.

I had to make her more confident, while training her to go outside to pee. Every evening before bed, to get her attention I would start by shaking the bunch of keys to the back door until she wandered through to the kitchen. Then I'd have the back door open as she arrived and would say 'out you go' while nodding my head in the direction of the door.

Once out there I stood on the path, put a treat up to her nose, then, when she went for it, I threw it onto the grass. At this point she would leap onto the grass and start sniffing out the treat. What this did was trigger her sniffing routine around the garden, which resulted in a pee at the end of it. The moment she went to pee I said 'go pee', and the moment she finished she got a treat.

Now when she wants to go out she comes and stares at me and I know she wants to go out for a pee. That took a couple of weeks, every evening, but it's done now. The rug and I are very glad.

It's not Groundhog Day

Don't think of training as something you need to get done before you can have a good time, something to be endured. Basic training is the foundation that your quality of life rests upon. Once the basics are learned you can move on to other things and training will become a lifelong trickle of learning as you go.

If you need to force your dog to do something she's already lost interest in, don't beat yourself up; come back and do it another time, especially if there's more interesting stuff happening for the dog elsewhere. Mix it up, try new tricks, learn recall in different places, play hide-and-seek so your dog has to find you (I do this when no one's looking so I don't look utterly crazy. Though I've just admitted it here. Oh well.)

When you need to get your dog's attention and recall him, make yourself the best thing in the vicinity. If you're in the park you're competing with scents and sounds your dog thinks are the best things ever – other dogs, fox scent, old chip packets, squirrels, hiding places, the nice lady with the Jack Russell who's always got bits of dried sausage in her pocket for him. The best thing my most excellent trainer and friend Debbie Peters ever told me (more on her in a minute) was to take a tube of cheese, or bits of sausage or chicken with me. 'Every time the dog comes back when you call her give her a lick of cheese or a piece of chicken. That way she'll know

there's a high reward treat for coming back.'

Hierarchy of rewards and jackpots

Scientific experiments have shown that animals will work harder if they aren't rewarded every time they do something for you.

At first, you should reward him every time he gets something right. Once he is used to doing things for rewards you can reduce the number he gets, and then taper off until he's never sure what he's going to get – a pat on the head and a 'well done' or a liver treat.

It is very important, though, to keep training sessions short. I wasn't kidding when I said you can teach a dog something while the kettle boils for tea. You don't want your dog to get tired or bored so don't overdo it and always end on a high note. If your dog walks away he's just not that into you right now, either because he's tired or there's something more exciting happening elsewhere. If he doesn't progress as you expect, remember *you* set a timeline of expectation, not him. You can always end with an easy trick when he does well so you finish with a positive experience.

Time to call in the professionals?

Owning a dog, for the first time especially, is like having a baby. You've babysat many times before but now you've got your own and you're in a different world. There are millions of people just like you, excited, cautious and a bit bewildered by their new four-legged charge. Everyone has an opinion, and you will be getting advice from all quarters, whether you like it or not, which is confusing in itself.

My experience – I really mean advice, of course (for what it's worth) – is to take the time to get to know your dog before seeking professional help, should you need it. Get to know how you all integrate in the household, learn each other's routines. After you've been together six months you'll look and think you were bonkers to do

some of the stuff you did.

You will also, by then, have a good idea of what you and your dog need help with. My trainer friend Debbie says that most rescue dogs are very well behaved for the first few weeks as they're effectively shut down and are just trying to cope with the new situation. Once they start to relax, that's when the idiosyncrasies start to emerge. This is called the Period of Disclosure – when their real behaviour and personality come out. Give it a few more weeks, while your dog lets it all hang out, then that's the time to call someone.

Puppies need socialising and training from a few weeks old – don't wait six months for them, as they have no baggage and will be open to every new experience you give them.

Finding a trainer and behaviourist

This is a tricky one. I found Debbie (www.school4dogs.com) by asking the receptionist at my vet's for a recommendation, then I checked her out as much as I could. Trainers and behaviourists don't have to be trained or regulated. Having said that, just because you're qualified doesn't make you any good, though Debbie most certainly is.

Her words of advice for finding yourself a trainer are: 'Look at their methods, not their qualifications. Opt for someone who uses positive, force-free methods.' In the end it will come down to who you think is right for you. Ask to go and watch them training, or observe a class they teach. Go with your gut. You will soon know if your dog is happy or not to train with them by their posture and body language, which you are now expert at!

A study, printed in the *Journal of Veterinary Behaviour* in March 2014 compared stress-related behaviours displayed by dogs trained using positive or negative reinforcement. When looking at walking on the lead and obeying the 'sit' command, the dogs trained using negative reinforcement (taking things away from the dog) demonstrated more stress signals than those trained positively – using praise for good behaviour (treats) and ignoring the unwanted behaviour (no treats). Those negatively reinforced had lowered body posture and less eye contact with their owners, for example. Dogs trained positively, on the other hand, showed increased attentiveness, confident body posture and better eye contact. Which is surely a far happier outcome for everyone. So much better to have a dog – whose sole aim in life is to please you – who is happy to work for reward, rather than one who's doing it to avoid punishment.

You're my first, my last, my everything

So, choose your dog wisely based on what you can reasonably expect to be able to give her in terms of time, space, exercise, mental stimulation and company. In the words of the late, great Barry White aka the Walrus of Love, you are everything to your dog. She looks up to you, is loyal to a fault and trusts you implicitly. Which gives you an awful lot of sway over how she turns out. It's also one hell of a responsibility. Make yourself the best thing in the room using positive methods of training and she'll do anything for you.

> If you can beat off all comers — treats, food and toys — when you step through the door at the end of the day, you've done a good job.

'Scratch it. Yeah, just there.'

So that's that

①

I started the business My Itchy Dog because we had an itchy dog, but I wrote the book for you.

Because along the way I have come to realise that, just like parents of human children, the large multinationals have grabbed us dog owners by the short and curlies and brainwashed us into believing that we must care for our charges in a prescribed fashion – one invented by them and their colossal marketing budgets.

They want us to fit into a dog-owning model which hardly existed 50 years ago. We must feed a certain food, and only that food. We must insure our pets to pay for the ever-expanding range of treatments available. We must seek a vet's help for every little thing. We must only administer *their* flea and worming treatments, and vaccinate at intervals set out by them and, if we don't, we're doing our dog harm. We must ride their gravy train. Every ounce of common sense, any dog care knowledge we possess, appears to count for nothing. We have been conned.

To add insult to injury, because the majority of purchasing decisions are made by women – 85%, roughly speaking – the advertising we're exposed to is of the guilt and fear variety, rather than the 'use this product and women will want to sleep with you' type aimed at men. This erodes our confidence even further.

So I'm here to shift some of that balance of power back to you, where it belongs. If you take only one thing from this book (though I hope you take a bit more – it's taken me flippin' ages to write!), remember this: *you know more than you think*. It's just been buried in the hype that's been shovelled onto you all these years. Stand back, take a good look at your dog and her lifestyle, then go with your gut.

Read the diet section again and work out how you want to feed your own dog. Dip in and out of the health section and find out how to treat those summer skin rashes, keep their joints in a puppy-like state of lubrication and your dog worm-free without ever again having to resort to a prescription wormer from the vet. If your great auntie Agatha had a recipe for hot spots she swore by, dredge it up from your memory and give it a go. What's the worst that can happen? Really not that much. It's probably got oats in it.

Once you have the right dog in your life, you're halfway there. Feed him the food that works for him. Add variety to his diet. Use good supplements and remedies bought from producers who are happy to share their knowledge and expertise with you. You can treat or prevent most problems using good food, exercise and great supplements so that, barring accidents, check-ups and the odd vaccination, you shouldn't need to visit the vet very often at all.

Couple that with good basic training and behaviour, a secure and loving place to live, and that's pretty much all your dog will ever need. That and you, of course, because you are the most important thing in your dog's world.

So sallie forth, my doggie friend, dare to dip your toe into the pond of common sense, relax about that rash! It doesn't need a skin scrape just yet – there are plenty of avenues to explore before you need to venture there. Crack him an egg onto the patio once in a while, slip her a broccoli stem when no one's looking.

But, perhaps most important of all, just be. Be together, enjoy each other's company, relax on a Sunday afternoon in the park, at the beach after work, or just on the sofa, preferably with a really good film on, the rain falling quietly against the window, a cup of tea and a biscuit for you and some totally horrible treat that he seems to like only because it smells awful.

Your dog will live a long and happy life. Then, when it's time, it may well be up to you to make the decision to let him go. And do it you will, with fortitude, dignity and lots of tears. But you will be able to do it – you will recover.

And you will have achieved a great thing, as a human being. You will have raised, taught, cajoled, trained, chased, cleaned up after, cared for, wiped fox poo off, shared a beautiful world with and loved a dog. And that is something to be mightily proud of and grateful for.

Do not disturb

◧ TOP DOG

SELFIES 📷

Share a photo of your own beloved pooch on instagram — @topdogselfie

Acknowledgements

Well, this has been an epic ride! "I'll have it written in six months"
I said to the ever patient and oh so lovely Aurea Carpenter. Two
years later and it's finally done. Thank you doesn't do it justice. But
to Victoria Marshallsay for calling to say "Ever thought of writing
a book?" and holding my hand throughout the whole process, and
to Aurea Carpenter and Rebecca Nicolson of Short Books for their
unswerving support, enthusiasm, encouragement and understanding,
I say thank you.

To Rupert Fawcett for agreeing to illustrate the book with his very
clever cartoons which capture a life lived with a dog so succinctly. To
Tiffany Mumford for her laid back days out with her camera and the
brilliant photography, and Jo Myler for her fab design. Eva Oyon, the
dog walker and trainer you see in the photos who, incidentally, got all
the dogs on a log at the same time www.evasdogs.blogspot.com.
Also to the happy volunteers – Chief, Boo, Jessie, Flash, Possum,
Caspar, Pushkin, Susan, Margot, Etta, Hugo, Cara, Luca, Bobbin,
Charlie et al – and a special mention for Malinki, the cheeky Jack
Russell on the cover.

I couldn't have written this book without the help, advice and
patience from the experts, in the face of some very silly questions.
Debbie Peters of School for Dogs, John Howie of Lintbells, Philip
Gazara of Verm-X, Julie Preston of Serendipity Herbals, Helen
Mayne of Feelwells, Mark Fox, lungworm expert at the Royal
Veterinary College, Richard Allport director of the Natural Medicine
Centre, the word vet doesn't begin to cover his job description,
and others who wish to remain nameless, for your help on diet, the
current state of the pet food industry, allergy testing, and other stuff.

As for those who supported and encouraged (and dragged) me
through getting the book finished, I owe you. Special thanks to
Tim and Sean for letting me hide in their lovely Spanish home (ten
thousand words that week, people) for making lovely dinners and
plying me with delicious gin. To Deb and Ging, and Heather for the
extra dog walks so I could stay at the keyboard, to Simon Collyer,
my 'work husband' for being a most brilliant mate and for all those
shoulder massages. You saved me a fortune at the osteopaths! Helen

O'Donnell and Helen Mayne, for reading, correcting and critiquing. David and James at coworking for letting me hide and get on with it. And last, but never ever least, thanks to Sophie, for everything.

A *massive* thanks as well to all my loyal and lovely customers who made my business what it is today and who made this book possible. If you hadn't kept telling me what you wanted and posing the hard questions it wouldn't be what it is and we wouldn't be where we are.

And finally, to the road testers Nikita, Ronnie, BB, Dave (RIP) and Pearl, our selfless dogs and cats. For their willingness to drop everything to try a new treat, their dedication when faced with a dinner different from the usual "Roast chicken and veg? If you *insist!*" And their sacrifice as we experiment, rubbing lotion after potion onto their bellies and wait eagerly for "that rash" to subside. Bless your furry, funny ways.

Index

a

acupuncture 135
additives 50, 55–81
Advocate 150, 176
Afghan hound 160
ageing see old age
aggression 195, 200–201
agrimony 137–8
air freshener 99, 117, 167
akita 161
allergies 91, 95, 98, 104, 124, 165–71, 172,
    177, 180
    immunotherapy injections 170–71
    testing for 165, 169–70
Allport, Richard 175
amino acids 42–3
anal glands, blocked 124, 126–7, 152
Andics, Attila 187–8
ankle problems 132–3
antibiotics 8, 92, 95, 118, 120
    long term use 154–6, 175
antibodies, testing 144–5
antlers 87, 130
anxiety 162–3, 200
Apple and Carrot Smoothie (recipe) 81
Apple and Cheese Treats (recipe) 73
apple cider vinegar 91, 95, 138
arthritis 91, 132–6
attention 27, 208

b

Bailey, Gwen 201–2
Banana and Peanut Butter Treats
    (recipe) 74
Banana Fruit Smoothies (recipe) 81
'Bark and Read' programme 24
barking 198, 201
basset hound 153
baths 199–200
Battersea Dogs Home 26
BB (author's dog) 9–10, 57, 92, 112, 153
beagle 119
Bedlington terrier 9, 96, 198

beds and bedding 27, 28, 29, 31, 138
beef 45, 166, 167
behaviour 191–215
behaviourists 213
Berns, Gregory 188
bichon frise 20, 22–3, 96
Billy No Mates 114, 158, 172, 176, 180
Bionic Biotic 126
birth 157–8
Birthday Cake (recipe) 78
bites 112, 124, 177
bladder 137–8
Blue Cross 146
body condition 140
body language 162, 193–4, 214
bones 39, 56, 57, 87–88, 129, 152–3, 198
    ground 84–5
boosters see vaccination
Border collie 22–3
Border terrier 20, 22–3
boredom 118–19, 195
borreliosis 101
borzoi 160
Boston terrier 26, 119, 161
bowel, weak 138
boxer 22–3, 119
brain-imaging 188
breath, bad 126, 128, 175
breed, choice of 7, 20–24, 26, 32, 197–8
British Association of Homeopathic
    Veterinary Surgeons (BAHVS) 144
broccoli 57, 87
bull terrier 22–3, 119
bulldog 22–3, 119, 160
burying food 198

c

cake 76–8
cancer 9, 53, 139, 179
Candida 96, 98–9, 115–16, 118, 124, 126
car travel 31, 198
carbohydrates 39, 42, 43, 46, 48, 96, 118,127
carpets 116, 167, 210

carrots 57, 87
cartilage erosion 133
cats 14, 163–4
cereal 39, 43, 44–8
cheese 39, 73
chewing 27, 28, 31, 129–30, 195, 197, 198, 210
Chicken and Vegetable Gluten-Free Stew (recipe) 61
Chicken Pupsicles (recipe) 71
Chicken Salad (recipe) 70
Chihuahua 22–3, 26, 160
children 19-20, 24, 26, 198, 202–5
chocolate 56
chondroitin 136
Christmas Dinner (recipe) 68
Cinnamon Trust 24
cleaning products 99, 110-11, 114, 116, 121, 167
coat condition see fur
coconut oil 10, 121–2, 138, 178–9
Coconut and Brewer's Yeast Treats (recipe) 75
cod liver oil 177
colitis 9, 126
collars 29, 31
collie 20, 22–3, 198, 207
colloidal silver 96, 153, 181
colour 38–9, 43, 48
communication 193–5
compulsive behaviour 163
concentration 127
conjunctivitis 153
constipation 126–7
cooking for your dog 55–81
coughing 115, 124
crates 27, 28, 31, 204
cross breeds 22–3, 32
cruciate ligament 132–3
CSJK9 117, 118, 130, 138, 156
cucumber 57, 89

d

dachshund 22–3, 161
dairy foods 39, 56, 166, 172
Dalmatian 119, 22–3
dander 167
day care 20, 144
deafness 162
death 163–4, 220
    causes of 160–61
deer antlers 87
DEFRA 173
demodex mites 105–6
depression 18, 186, 195
Dermacton 122, 138
dermatitis 98, 115
destructiveness 196–7
diabetes 139, 151–2
diarrhoea 125–6, 149
diet see food
digestion 10, 39, 125–7, 175
digging 198
disc herniation 132–3
Discover Dogs 26
distemper vaccine 142
D-Limonene 121
Doberman 160
dog racing 188
dog walkers 20, 24, 119, 187
Doggie con Carne (recipe) 69
dog-proofing the home 28
Dogs Trust 20, 26, 146
dominance 193
Dorwest 119, 126-7, 131, 138, 157, 174, 180
dribbling 129
dry food see kibble
dust mites 103–4, 124, 166, 167, 172
dysplasia see elbow problems; hip problems

e

ears
    blockages 96
    cleaning 93, 97, 181

and diet 36, 126
hair in 96, 98
hearing loss 162
infections 9, 26, 36, 93–8
itchy 124, 165
mites 96, 104–5, 181
echinacea 10, 95, 122, 171, 175
eggs 39, 57, 88
Ekoneem 106, 111–12, 116–17, 122, 181
elbow problems 132–3
elderly dogs *see* old age
elimination diets 167–9
emotional well-being 185–8
energy 36, 39, 126–7, 196
enteritis 127
epilepsy 137
essential oils 121
European Pet Food Industry Federation
    (FEDIAF) 41
evening primrose oil 177
exercise 20, 28, 37, 127, 132, 161, 195; *see*
    also walking
eyes 26, 126, 181, 153-4
cleaning 153–4
running 115, 124, 153, 165, 177

f

Farm Foods Antlers 130
fashion 20, 26
fats 39, 42, 43, 46–8, 56, 58, 139, 152
fear 195, 201–2
Feelwells 126
Fenton YouTube video 207
fibre 42, 43
fireworks 119
fish 47, 57–8, 88
oils 135, 173, 176
tinned 177–8
Fish Friday (recipe) 64
fleas 98–100, 121, 124, 148, 167
combing out 106
herbal prevention 10, 92, 114–15, 122,
    176, 180

in the home 110–11, 114
during pregnancy 158
floors 116–17, 167, 210
flyball 20
folliculitis 124
food 35–89
allergies to 166–70
appetite 149, 161
changing your dog's diet 10, 52–3,
    139–41
cost 41, 51, 83
giving leftovers and other human food
    58, 87, 204
home cooked 55–81
ingredients 39, 41–8, 118, 128
kibble (dried food) 35, 37, 39, 43, 46,
    52, 85
labelling 43–52, 169
quantities 85
raw 83–6, 127–8, 172
safety 52, 56
types and brands 27, 38–53, 219
variety in 27, 57, 88–9, 128, 139
vegetarian 178
wet 37, 43
see also obesity
forgetfulness 161–3
fostering 24
Four Seasons 151
foxes 88, 105
fragrances 121, 167
Frontline 176
fruit 56, 57
fungal problems 96, 99, 115-16, 171–3, 177,
    181
fur 10, 39, 115, 126-7, 161, 176
dry and coarse 149
loss 105–6, 156, 171–2, 175
stained 124
furniture chewing 197, 210

g

Game of Thrones 20, 197
gastritis 125, 127, 161
gastrointestinal disorders 161, 165
German shepherd 22–3, 26, 119
gestation period 157
gingivitis 130
glucosamine 135
golden retriever 22–3
Gordon setter 161
Great Dane 153, 160–61
green-lipped mussel extract 136
greyhound 22–3, 32, 139, 161, 196
grief 164–5
grooming 99, 121
growling 200–201
guarding 198
gums 128, 130

h

hair loss 106, 124
harnesses 31
harvest mites 105, 124
hay fever 115, 124, 177
health benefits of owning a dog 18–19
Health Protection Agency (HPA) 101
health scares 42
hearing loss 162
heart disease 9, 130, 139, 160
herbs 176
herding instincts 207
Hills 41
hip problems 26, 132–3
Hold It! 138
homeopathy 144–6, 158, 159
Honey's Real Dog Food 84
hookworms 149
hormonal disorders 119, 136–7
house-training 17, 28, 136, 210
How Dogs Love Us 188
hunting instincts 207
husky 20, 197
hydrotherapy 135

hyperthyroidism 129, 175

i

IAMS 41
ID tags 29, 31
immune system 35, 39, 95, 105–6, 115, 142, 171, 176
immunisation see vaccination
immunotherapy injections 170–71, 172
incontinence 136–8, 152, 162–3
Indorex spray 110
insulin 151
insurance 8, 144, 219
intestines 125–6, 161
intolerances 165
iodine 114, 175
Irish wolfhounds 161
itching and scratching 9, 36, 83, 86, 91, 98, 115, 118, 124, 165, 172, 175, 177, 181

j

Jack Russell terrier 17, 32, 160
Jerky (recipe) 72
joints 36, 132, 135, 175, 181; *see also* arthritis
Journal of Nutrition 151
jumping, difficulties with 133
jumping up 208

k

K9 Rescue Bulgaria 29
Keepers Mix 126–7
Kennel Club 20–24, 26
kibble (dried food) 35, 37, 39, 43, 46, 52, 85
kidney problems 130, 137, 163–4
knee problems 132–3
Kong toys 119

l

Labrador retriever 20, 22–3
lactose 39

lameness 132–6
leads 28, 31, 204
leave command 210
leaving dogs home alone 14, 17, 20, 27, 29, 121, 186, 195
legal obligations 27
lemon balm 114–15
lhasa apso 22–3
lick granuloma 124
licking 129, 133, 137
ligaments 132–3
Lintbells 118, 126, 135, 153, 174
liver 130
Liver Cake (recipe) 76
loneliness 18
Lonsdale, Tom 86
love 18, 27
loyalty 14, 17, 32
lungworms 148–50, 158
lupus 119
lurchers 17, 89, 139, 196
Lyme disease 101–3

m

malamutes 20, 197
malassezia 10, 116, 170
Maltese 160
mange 10, 166, 170, 180
    mites 105, 116, 124
marrowbones 130
Mars 41, 51
McKeith, Gillian 152
McMillan, Franklin D. 185
meat 42–3, 46–7, 57–8, 88
    derivatives 44–8, 51
    and food labelling law 44–5
medications 8, 156
memory 161
Mental Health and Wellbeing in Animals 185
mental well-being 185–8
metabolic disorders 119
micro-chipping 29

Milbemax 176
milk 39, 56
minerals 39, 42, 43, 46–8, 50, 176
missing dogs 29
mites 10, 96, 98, 103–6, 124, 158, 180
    herbal prevention 114–15, 122
mobility 181
moods 199
moulting 180
    non-moulting breeds 96, 98
MRI scans 187–8
muffin recipes 66–7
musculoskeletal conditions 161
mussels, green-lipped 136
My Itchy Dog 9, 18, 86, 98, 117, 219

n

nail clipping 199–200
National Vaccination Month 146
Natural Instinct 84
Nature Diet 53, 56
Nature's Menu 84
neem oil 10, 95-6, 106, 111–14, 118, 121–2, 177, 180-81
    contraceptive properties 159
    shampoo 106, 111, 115, 122
negative reinforcement 214
neglect, signs of 139
nerve damage 137
Nestlé Purina 41, 51
neurological conditions 137, 161
neutering 137
Newfoundland 160
Nikita (author's dog) 10, 28, 29–32, 57, 88–9, 112, 128, 131, 153, 165, 188, 196, 198, 203
Nina Ottoson 118–19
Northern Inuit 197
nose, running 115, 124, 165, 177
nosodes 144–6
nutraceuticals 42, 50
nutrition 37, 39, 42, 55, 154, 176

o

oats 57, 121, 152–3
Obama, Barack 20
obedience techniques 208–10
obesity 9, 36, 133, 139–41, 149, 152, 162
O'Donnell, Helen 188
offal 84–5
oils 39, 46–8, 176–9
old age 143, 160–65
omega oils 10, 50, 115, 136, 176–8, 180
onions 56, 58
opinions and advice 189–90, 213
organic food 42
osteoarthritis 132–3
O'Tom Tick Twister 109, 181

p

pack behaviour 193
pain 132, 176, 185, 200–201
Panacur 151
pancreatitis 9, 39, 151–2
panting 98
parabens 117, 121
parasites 8, 28, 88, 98, 148, 158, 166
parenting 188–9
parvovirus 127, 142
paws, itchy 124
Pawz boots 116–17
PDSA 146
peanut butter 74
Peanut Butter Smoothie (recipe) 81
peeing 8, 10, 28, 29, 136–8, 162–3, 196, 210
Pet Head 117
pet shops 42, 84, 174
Peters, Debbie 211, 213
phtalates 117, 121
physiotherapy 135
Picnic Muffins (recipe) 66
placebo effect 144
plaque 129
Plaque Off 130
playing, with other dogs 27, 28
poisons 56

pollen 166, 170, 181
poo 8, 28, 83, 126-7, 152, 167; see also diarrhoea
Pooch & Mutt 126
poodle 22–3, 96, 119
Pork and Potato Stew (recipe) 60, 167
Portuguese water dog 20
positive reinforcement 187, 201, 214
potatoes 56
prebiotics 126, 156
pregnancy 151, 156–9
probiotics 115, 118, 121-2, 126, 156
ProDen 130
protein 39, 42–3, 46, 85
psyllium 127
pug 20, 22–3, 26, 161
pulsatilla 159
punishment 210
puppies 26, 143, 150-51, 157-9, 201-2, 213
puppy farms 20, 188
Pure Dog Stag Bar 130
puzzles 118

r

rabies 143, 145, 171
raisins 56
rashes 124, 179
raspberry leaf 137–8, 157, 159
raw food 31, 37, 83–6, 89, 127–8, 172
rawhide 87
ready meals 55
recall 211–12
recipes 60–81
regurgitation 125
rescue dogs 20, 24, 26, 213
Rescue Remedy 159
respiratory problems 160, 165
rewards 209, 210, 211–12
rhubarb 56
rice 57, 167, 169
ringworm 124
Ronnie (author's dog) 9–10, 57, 198
rosemary 115, 121

Rottweiler 20, 22–3
roundworms 148–9
routines 163, 213
RSPCA 139, 146
running 27, 133, 207

s

safety 27, 28
sage 115, 121
Salmon and Vegetable Fishcakes
    (recipe) 69
salt 56, 58–9
sarcoptes mites 105
scavenging 127, 195
schnauzer 20, 22–3
scratches 112, 177
scratching see itching and scratching
scullcap 159
seatbelts 31
seaweed 47, 114, 129, 131, 175
senility 162–3
separation anxiety 197
shampoos 10, 99, 115, 117, 118, 121
shar pei 161
shih-tzu 22–3, 119
shoes, chewing 210
show dogs 26
showers 199
sign language 162, 194
sitting 198, 214
Skin and Bones (recipe) 62
skin colour 124
skin problems 98, 115-24, 129, 137-8, 171,
    176, 179-81; see also itching and
    scratching
Skinny Cream 115
Skinny Dip shampoo 106
Skinny Spray 111
sleep 195, 204
smell, sense of 38
smelliness 124, 126, 177
smoothies 80–81
sneezing 124, 177

sniffing 27, 38, 195, 204, 211
social life, and dog ownership 18–19
socialisation 195, 201–2, 208, 213
sodium lauryl/laureth sulphates 115, 117,
    121
spaniels 20, 22–3, 26, 153
spaying 137, 159
spine damage 137
St Bernard 161
St John's wort 175
Staffordshire bull terrier 20, 22–3
Stag Bars 31
staring 161, 204
staying 198
steroids 8, 120, 138, 154-6, 172, 175
stomach upsets 125-7, 154, 157
stress 18, 19, 29, 95, 118–19, 121, 124, 214
sugars 45–6, 48, 56, 96, 118, 121, 167
supplements 9, 50, 122, 133, 135-6, 171–81
sweating 98
sweet potatoes 57, 169

t

tapeworms 99, 148–9
tear staining 154
teeth 10, 36, 128–31, 161
tendons 132
terriers 17, 20, 22–3, 160
Thornit powder 96, 181
thrush 154, 156
thyroid 129, 175
ticks 10, 98, 101–3, 106, 167, 180
    herbal prevention 114–15, 122
    during pregnancy 158
    removing 109, 181
titre test 92, 144–5
toothbrushes 131
toothpaste 131, 180
Toxocara 148
toys 28, 204
training 26, 198, 207-14
travelling 31, 119, 198
treats 9, 31, 47, 86–7, 89, 165, 204, 211–12

recipes 71–8
tricks 209, 211, 213
Tuna Cake (recipe) 77
Turkey, Pear Mash and Oat Muffins
    (recipe) 67
tweezers 109, 181
Twilight 197

u

urinary problems 136–8
urtica urens 158, 159

v

vaccination 92, 141–6, 219
valerian 159, 175
vegetable oils 176
vegetable supplements 138
vegetables 39, 43, 45, 46–8, 57–9, 88, 152
vegetarian diet 178
Veggie Seedy Patties (recipe) 72
Verm-X 10, 150–51, 158, 172, 176, 180
Vetbed 138
Veterinary Medicines Directorate 173
vets 8, 83, 91, 219–20
    fees 8, 35, 144, 151
    home visits 164
vinegar 91, 95, 138
Vitamin B Special (recipe) 81
vitamins 55–6, 157
vomiting 125, 165

w

walking 15–19, 132, 195-6, 214
    off-lead 187, 207
    see also exercise
washing 138
water 27, 127
weeing 8, 10, 28, 29, 136–8, 162–3, 196, 210
weight *see* obesity
Weimaraner 22–3, 161
Welfare of Animals Act 2006 27
West Highland terrier 20, 22–3, 26, 119,

153, 154
wet food 37, 39
wet wipes 117
wheatgerm oil 157
wheezing 115, 124, 177
whelping 157–8
Whimzees 130
whining 163
whippet 22–3
whipworms 149
wind 126
working dogs 195
World Small Animal Veterinary
    Association (WSAVA) 143
worms 10, 92, 121, 124, 148–51, 158, 180,
    219–20
    egg counts 149–51, 158
    herbal prevention and treatment 122,
    148, 150, 158, 176

x

xylitol 56, 131

y

yeast 57, 75
Yorkshire terrier 20, 22–3, 153, 160
Yumega Plus 115, 177, 180
Yumove 181
YumPro 96, 115, 118, 126, 135, 181

Author biography

KATE BENDIX worked for many years in television documentaries. In 2009, she jacked it all in, embraced poverty, and started her own business My Itchy Dog. Being an experienced broadcaster and journalist, she still loves the sound of her own voice and features on radio shows and in dog magazines whenever she can get past security. She lives by the sea.